Prioritize Your Potential

Maximize Your Strengths, Achieve Your Goals, Transform Your Life

Compiled by

Sharvette Mitchell

Erika Brooks • Dr. Nina Copeland • Ifedayo Greenway
Dr. Valarie Harris • Pastor Kathleen Kim Moore
Lynn Lewis • Edwinette Moses • Jean Tillery
Wanda L. Washington • Dana Wilson

Mitchell Productions, LLC

Prioritize Your Potential

Paperback ISBN# 979-8-9876197-8-0
Hardback ISBN# 979-8-9876197-9-7
eBook ISBN# 979-8-9995033-0-5

Published by:
Mitchell Productions, LLC
www.Mitchell-Productions.com

Back Cover Photography
Kimie James

Anthology Editor
Chandra Sparks Splond, M.S.E.
www.chandrasparkssplond.com

Book Design and Layout by Brand It Beautifully™
www.branditbeautifully.com

The lyrics to "I Am A Promise" are used with permission from Capital CMG Publishing.

Scriptures marked NIV are taken from the NEW INTERNATIONAL VERSION (NIV): Scripture taken from THE HOLY BIBLE, NEW INTERNATIONAL VERSION ®. Copyright© 1973, 1978, 1984, 2011 by Biblica, Inc.™. Used by permission of Zondervan.

Scriptures marked NKJV are taken from the NEW KING JAMES VERSION (NKJV): Scripture taken from the NEW KING JAMES VERSION®. Copyright© 1982 by Thomas Nelson, Inc. Used by permission. All rights reserved.

Scriptures marked NLT are taken from the HOLY BIBLE, NEW LIVING TRANSLATION (NLT): Scriptures taken from the HOLY BIBLE, NEW LIVING TRANSLATION, Copyright© 1996, 2004, 2007 by Tyndale House Foundation. Used by permission of Tyndale House Publishers, Inc., Carol Stream, Illinois 60188. All rights reserved. Used by permission.

Contents

To my mother, Bettye J. Mitchell, who nurtures space for me to dream with grace, and to my sister, Kym Leonard, who reminds me daily of the power of sisterhood and support. You are my "true north" and my biggest fans.

Introduction

Let's be real...many of us wear a lot of hats.

You're a professional. Maybe a spouse. Maybe a parent. Maybe a business owner navigating team meetings in one moment and school pickup in the next. You're managing responsibilities, showing up strong, and doing what needs to be done. But deep down, you might be wondering...

When is it my turn to prioritize myself?

As a leadership consultant and full-time business owner, I've had countless conversations with people, just like you—high achievers, impact-makers, visionaries—who secretly feel stuck in a life that looks successful on paper but feels incomplete in purpose. We get so good at pushing forward that we start ignoring the quiet nudge calling us to pause or dream bigger.

This book collaboration is for that person.

Their stories, life lessons, and strategies are not just inspirational; they are instructional.

If you've ever felt like you're meant for more but life keeps getting in the way, you're in the right place. This book is your mirror and your permission slip all wrapped in one!

So exhale. You don't have to have it all figured out.

But you do have to be willing to move to the priority lane in your life.

Here's a recommended way to read this book...

This is not the kind of book collaboration you rush through. It's the kind you sit with.

Each chapter stands on its own, written by a woman who has walked through her own version of the pause, that season where life forces you to stop, reassess, and decide if you're really living in alignment with your potential.

You can read this cover to cover, or jump to the chapter that speaks to you first. Either way, I encourage you to read with a highlighter nearby and perhaps a journal within reach. There are gems and gold here. Lessons. Confirmations. Invitations.

If something stirs you, sit with it. If a sentence hits a little too close, say... "Ouch!" but lean in. That's usually where the growth begins.

Perhaps you're rediscovering your dreams, launching something new, or learning to believe in yourself again—use this book as a tool.

And most of all, let this be the moment you stop waiting for the "right time."

Your next move doesn't have to be perfect. It can be shaky and uncertain. It just has to be yours.

Sharvette Mitchell
CEO of Mitchell Productions
Visionary Author and Compiler of Prioritize Your Potential

Epic Moves
Seven Ways to Prioritize Your Potential and Reignite Your Dreams
Jean Tillery

The Truth About Potential

There's a moment many women know all too well. We look around at a life that seems successful on paper but doesn't feel quite full. We've checked the boxes, kept the plates spinning, met everyone else's needs, but we can feel deep down that we're not operating at full capacity. We've got more to give, more to become, and more to dream, but we don't know how to unlock it.

That ache that you feel? That's not failure. That's potential trying to get your attention.

Here's how I define it: *Potential is the sum of your untapped capacity, talents, dreams, and drive—the combination of what you can do, what you desire to do, what you were created for, and what the world needs from you.*

It's the space between where you are and what's possible when your values, vision, and actions align.

In business, prioritizing potential doesn't just mean scaling faster, growing bigger, or earning more, it means becoming the kind of leader, creator, or visionary who is lit from within and building something sustainable, impactful, and deeply fulfilling.

To prioritize your potential means to be wildly intentional. It means making space for growth, saying yes to the things that expand you, and closing the door on what no longer serves you. It means listening to that still, small voice that is whispering, *"There's more for you. Don't stop now."*

I haven't learned this from books or seminars but from lived experience. From having it all together and falling apart. From chasing goals and then finding myself lost in the process. From setting out to promote my business to discovering the healing I didn't know I needed.

A Road Trip, a Breakdown, and a Breakthrough

In 2021, I packed up my car and took off on a five-and-a-half-week solo road trip across twenty-two states. I didn't get far on that trip before realizing it was less about business and more about healing.

I had spent years running a gauntlet of health issues, long COVID, the fog of menopause, and the constant busyness of building a life around other people's needs, trying to hold everything and everyone together. The truth is, I didn't even realize how much of me I had lost in the process.

After becoming a Certified Dream Manager and developing the foundation of my own program, I knew it was time to walk my talk. For more than twelve years, a cross-country road trip had been sitting on my own dream list, waiting for the right time, the right season, the right permission.

I finally realized, there is no perfect time. And what better way to launch a dream-centered business than by living out one of my biggest dreams?

So, I packed my bags, hit the road, and used the journey to embody what I'd be asking of my clients—to say yes to possibility, to live with intention, and to take the dream off the paper and into the world.

Somewhere during the 8,181 miles, I started to feel pieces of myself return. I saw new places and experienced new things. I met new people. I wrote. I cried. I rested. I prayed. Somewhere out there on the open road, I remembered something powerful: My dreams still mattered. Not in a someday, maybe later, once-the-kids-are-grown kind of way. What unfolded during those five-and-a-half weeks was more than a trip. It was a living example of what happens when you prioritize your potential and dare to dream again.

And so I ask you, as a woman, an entrepreneur, a dreamer: What would it look like for you to finally prioritize your potential?

If that is what you want, you must do it on purpose. It doesn't happen by accident, and it's never too late to start.

Here are seven epic moves I've learned to live by—in my life, in my business, and in the lives of the women I work with.

Epic Move #1: Write It Down

"A dream not written down is just a wish."

— Unknown

It all begins with clarity. Not hustle, not perfection, not five-year plans... Just the courage to get honest about what you really want.

I can't tell you how many women I have heard say:

- "I used to have dreams, but I can't remember them anymore."
- "Everything I want feels selfish or unrealistic."
- "I don't even know where to begin."

And I always say, "Begin by writing it down."

Write it messy. Write it wild. Write it without editing or judging or figuring out how it will all happen. Just put it on paper. Want to learn a new skill? Write it down. Want to travel to Italy? Write it down. Want to start a business? Write it down. Want to feel confident in your body again? Write it down.

When you write it down, you name it. And when you name it, you claim it.

Personal Story

I first heard about the Dream Manager program in 2009. The program starts with you making a list of one hundred dreams—big ones, silly ones, sacred ones.

My first dream list had things like *take a helicopter ride* and *host a women's retreat*. Others were as simple as *make homemade soap* or *take an art class*.

Some of those dreams have already come true. Others are still in process. But all of them matter—because they are evidence of who I am and who I'm becoming.

Action Step

Grab a notebook and set a timer for fifteen minutes. Without filtering or overthinking, write down every dream, desire, and possibility that comes to mind. Aim for twenty-five things. Don't stop to figure out the "how." Just write.

Journal Prompt

If nothing was off-limits—no limitations of time, money, energy, or age —what would I love to experience, create, give, or become?

Epic Move #2: Choose Target Dreams

> *"You can do anything—but not everything all at once."*
>
> — David Allen

You don't need a ten-year plan—you need a next right step. I have my clients choose four target dreams each year—at least one short-term dream (within the next six months), one medium (one to two years), and one long-term dream (three to five years), and focus their energy there. Target dreams help you move from scattered to strategic.

Personal Story

When working on my 2025 dream list, I had dozens of dreams swirling in my head for my Epic Living with Jean business—host retreats, grow my podcast, write another book, start a membership community, host a summit, partner with women's organizations, and more.

And guess what? Each of those things still excite me. If I had tried to do them all at once, I would've drowned in decision fatigue and burnt out before anything had a chance to bloom. Instead, I got clear on my target dreams:

- One of my short-term dreams: Launch the 5-Day Dream Activation Challenge + 30-Day Dream List Builder.
- One of my long-term dreams: Write and publish a children's book and grow a seven-figure dream-centered brand.

When I chose to prioritize those specific dreams, I stopped spinning and started moving. Each action became more focused. Each decision had a filter.

Target dreams give your energy a direction, and direction matters more than speed.

Coaching Insight

So many of us feel stuck, not because we lack motivation, but because we lack focus. Your dreams are worthy, but they need your full attention to grow. Choosing one or two at a time doesn't mean giving up on the rest. It means building a foundation strong enough to hold them all.

Action Step

Look at your current dream list. Circle one dream you could begin working on in the next three to six months—something that excites you *and* feels achievable. Then, choose one dream that will take longer—two to five years—and write it somewhere visible.

Now, ask yourself: What is one step I can take this week toward each of these dreams?

Journal Prompt

Which dream lights me up right now? Which dream feels like a long-game vision that's calling me forward? What would shift in my life if I gave each of them real space and attention this year?

Epic Move #3: Guard Your Energy Like It's Currency

Time is precious, but energy is priceless.

You already know that your time is valuable, but here's the real game-changer: Your energy is even more important.

Time can be scheduled. Tasks can be delegated. But energy? It's your most finite, non-renewable resource, and when you spend it on the wrong things, it costs you more than you realize.

You can't live in your potential if you're constantly running on empty. As women, we've been conditioned to believe that being exhausted is a badge of honor. That saying yes is kind. That doing "all the things" is how you prove your worth.

But here's what I've learned: Sometimes the most powerful way to prioritize your potential is to stop giving your energy to things that don't align with it.

Personal Story

There was a season when I said yes to everything: collaborations that didn't feel aligned, volunteer roles that drained me, social obligations that left me depleted, and projects I didn't have the capacity to carry. I was exhausted, distracted, and constantly behind on my own dreams. I believe that was a lot of what contributed to my health problems over the years. It wasn't until I started treating my energy like a currency and asking, *Is this how I want to spend it?* that things began to shift. Now, I filter decisions through a simple lens:

- Does this align with my mission?
- Will this energize me or deplete me?
- Is this mine to carry, or am I picking it up out of guilt or habit?

I still give generously, but now, it comes from overflow, not obligation.

Coaching Insight

Boundaries are not selfish...they're sacred.

Saying no to the things that drain you makes room for the things that grow you. You're not just protecting your schedule; you're protecting your potential.

If something (or someone) consistently leaves you feeling drained, resentful, or out of alignment, it's time to reevaluate where your energy is going.

Action Step

Make a list of your top five current commitments—personal or professional. For each one, ask yourself:

- Is this fueling me or draining me?
- Is this aligned with my dreams and values?
- What would it look like to release or restructure this?

Then, commit to eliminating or reducing just *one* energy leak this week.

Journal Prompt

Where is my energy going—and what would it feel like to reclaim some of it for the things that truly matter?

Epic Move #4: Build Before You're Ready

You don't need confidence to take the first step—just courage.

Let's get real for a second: No one *ever* feels completely ready to chase a big dream. We wait for more time, more money, more experience, more clarity, but the truth is, clarity rarely comes before action. It most often comes through action.

You don't need to have it all figured out. You just need to move. Start scrappy. Start small. Start scared if you must. Just start. Building before you feel ready is not reckless. It's faithful. It says, "I trust this dream enough to take the first step, even if the path isn't fully clear."

Personal Story

When I launched my first 5-Day Dream Activation Challenge, I didn't have a team or a fancy funnel. I had a vision, a deep belief in what I was teaching, and a willingness to figure it out as I went. Was it perfect? Nope. Did I learn a ton? Absolutely. Did it help real women reconnect with their dreams and take bold steps toward their potential? Yes, and that's what mattered most.

Now that same challenge is part of the foundation of my business, and it's impacted dozens of lives—because I chose to build before I felt fully ready.

Coaching Insight

Your dreams aren't waiting for perfection; they are waiting for permission. Stop putting them on pause while you try to "get your act together." What if you gave yourself permission to grow while you go? You will get better. You will find your rhythm. You will tweak and refine. But none of that can happen until you begin.

Action Step

Pick one idea you've been sitting on: the book, the podcast, the product, the event—and ask, what's the smallest, scrappiest way I can start this now? Then...do it.

Send the email. Record the first voice memo. Make the outline. Book the date.

Build before you feel ready, and you'll be amazed at how ready you become.

Journal Prompt

If I trusted that I didn't need to be perfect, what would I start building today?

Epic Move #5: Design Systems That Support Your Potential

Structure doesn't stifle your dreams—it sustains them.

Dreams are beautiful. But dreams without support? They fizzle. One of the most powerful (and overlooked) ways to prioritize your potential is to design systems that make space for your dreams to grow. Not just ideas floating in the ether, but tangible habits, tools, and structures that carry your intentions from inspiration to execution. This is where so many women, especially visionaries and creatives, get stuck. You have the ideas. The passion. The heart. But the chaos of day-to-day life keeps stealing your focus.

That's where systems come in. And no, I'm not talking about turning your life into a military operation or building color-coded spreadsheets (unless you love that sort of thing—in which case, go wild).

I'm talking about gentle but powerful containers that help your potential thrive.

Personal Story

When I first launched my Dream Manager programs, I quickly realized that inspiration alone wasn't going to sustain them. I needed systems—not just to manage clients or emails, but to support *me*.

So I started small:

- A weekly block in my calendar for Dream List Builder work
- A simple customer relationship management tool to organize contacts and follow-ups
- An Opus Clip system to repurpose video content
- Folders in Canva to finally stop the design chaos (well, sort of)

These weren't fancy, but they gave my ideas structure. They created a rhythm. And they reminded me that honoring my potential wasn't just about big leaps, it was about building sustainable flow.

Coaching Insight

Systems don't remove the soul from your dream—they free you up to focus on what matters most. When you're constantly in reaction mode, you burn energy just trying to stay afloat. But when you have systems—even simple ones—you create margin, consistency, and a sense of peace.

Remember, you don't need a system for everything, but you do need a few that work for you.

Action Step

Pick one area of your life or business that feels chaotic. Ask:

- What's one small system I can create to make this easier?
- Do I need a recurring calendar block, a checklist, a meal plan, or a workflow?

Start small. Repeat. Refine.

Journal Prompt

What part of my dream feels the most chaotic or unsustainable? What kind of system or rhythm would help it grow with less stress and more joy?

Epic Move #6: Find Your Tribe

The voices around you shape the voice within you.

You were never meant to do this alone. One of the sneakiest threats to your potential isn't failure...it's isolation. When you're surrounded by people who don't dream, who play small, who question your vision every time you try to grow, it's like trying to run a marathon with ankle weights.

You need people who see you, get you, and speak life over your dreams. You need people who remind you who you are on the days you forget. You need a tribe.

Personal Story

When I first started putting Epic Living with Jean into the world, not everyone got it. Some thought "dream coaching" sounded fluffy. Others questioned if people would really invest in something so...intangible.

But you know who never doubted? My tribe. They didn't just nod politely, they cheered. They connected me with others. They gave me space to process, reminded me of my mission, and spoke life over every little seed I was planting.

Without them, some of those dreams might've stayed buried.

Your potential is precious, and it deserves to be nurtured by people who believe in your capacity to become everything you're called to be.

Coaching Insight

The right people will never shrink your dreams; they will expand them.

If you've been surrounded by doubt, judgment, comparison, or fear-based advice, then it's time to change your circle. Find the people who clap when you win, sit with you when you cry, and remind you that your dreams are not too big.

Action Step

Make a list of the five people you spend the most time with. Ask yourself:

- Do they believe in me?
- Do they lift me up or wear me out?
- Are they living in alignment with their own potential?

Then take action. Spend time with your tribe. And if you don't have one yet, start looking. They're out there, dreaming, too.

Journal Prompt

Who are the people who reflect the best parts of me—the ones who believe in my dreams even when I doubt myself? How can I deepen those connections this season?

Epic Move #7: Surrender the Timeline, Not the Dream

Delayed doesn't mean denied.

This one is for the woman who thought she'd be farther along by now. The one who keeps showing up, keeps hoping, keeps doing the work, and still hasn't seen the breakthrough she's been praying for. It's for the woman who whispers, "Maybe it's just not meant to be."

Let me say this gently but clearly: Just because your dream hasn't happened on your timeline doesn't mean it's not still in motion.

Dreams often take longer than we think they will, but they also go deeper than we imagined they could.

Personal Story

In October 2022, I was finally ready to take some big steps in my business. My youngest graduated from college, and my daughter's wedding had just passed. Life felt open and aligned. I headed to Texas for a few speaking events, loaded up with fresh energy, new goals, and a clear path forward.

Then, on October 31, everything changed.

My husband suffered a brain aneurysm while traveling out of state. For over six hours, I knew something was wrong but had no contact with him. I left Texas and drove toward the last place I knew he'd been—Spartanburg, South Carolina.

By the time I located him, he had been transferred to a hospital in Greenville, where he spent thirty-two days in the Neuro-ICU. I lived out of a hotel room, holding my breath between doctor updates, trying to stay strong while everything I had planned vanished overnight.

All those goals? On pause. All those dreams? Derailed. But even then, something in me knew that this wasn't the end of the story. The timeline had shifted, but the dream hadn't died. I just had to hold on through the storm.

Coaching Insight

Dreams don't always wait for you to feel fully ready. Sometimes, they show up before you think you're prepared, and yet, they're still right on time.

That cross-country road trip I'd dreamed about for more than twelve years? It didn't happen the way I had originally imagined. The circumstances weren't perfect. The timing felt uncertain. But when the moment came, there was no doubt: It was time. Looking back, I can see it was exactly what I needed—even if I hadn't planned it that way.

So don't wait to feel one hundred percent ready. Dreams have a way of meeting you right where you are and unfolding in ways that surprise you. Stay open. Stay curious. Stay in motion.

Action Step

Think of a dream that's been slow to unfold. Instead of asking, "Why hasn't it happened yet?" ask, "Who am I becoming as I wait for it?" Then write down one way you can nurture the dream, even if it's not happening right now.

Journal Prompt

What dream have I been tempted to give up on—and what would it look like to surrender the timeline but stay faithful to the vision?

Note on Small Dreams

Not every dream has to be a business launch or a book deal. Some of the most powerful momentum comes from honoring the smaller dreams—baking bread from scratch, finishing that craft project you started three years ago, having a weekly coffee date with your best friend, or finally printing the photos from your last vacation. These dreams matter because you matter—and they bring joy, creativity, and healing to everyday life. Prioritizing your potential includes honoring what makes your soul smile.

So, whether you're dreaming of a TED Talk or learning to knit a scarf, write it down, speak it out loud, and take the next step.

Epic Pitfalls: What Gets in the Way of Prioritizing Your Potential

It's not always the big obstacles that derail us—it's the quiet lies we start to believe.

As women with dreams, it's easy to assume that what holds us back is a lack of time, money, or resources. But in my experience—both personally and with my clients—the biggest roadblocks are more subtle.

Here are three common pitfalls that can quietly sabotage your potential if you're not careful:

1. **"I don't have time."** Let's be honest: Time is tight. But often, this belief isn't about hours on the clock. It's about how much permission we've given ourselves to prioritize what matters. When we claim even small windows of focused time for our dreams, we prove that they matter.
2. **"I don't know what I want."** This often comes from years of serving everyone else. It's not that we don't have dreams, it's that we've forgotten how to hear them. But the truth is, you don't have to figure it all out right away. You just need to get curious and start listening again.
3. **"It's too late."** This one breaks my heart—and it's a lie. I've watched women in their fifties, sixties, and beyond write books, start businesses, find love, launch nonprofits, and finally live the life they've always dreamed of. Your potential doesn't expire. It just evolves.

Recognize these lies. Replace them with truth. And keep going, because the only thing more powerful than your dream is your decision to believe in it.

You Are the Dream

I want to leave you with a moment—one I think about often.

I was somewhere in the middle of nowhere, early in my cross-country road trip. The road stretched wide in front of me. My playlist was on. My journal was full of dreams I hadn't dared say out loud in years.

And suddenly, I started to cry. Not because I was sad, but because I realized: I was living a dream I had written down more than a decade ago.

No one handed it to me. I didn't wait until I had all the answers. I just decided to trust the voice inside me that said, "It's time." And friend, maybe that's where you are now. Maybe you've been waiting for permission. Maybe you've been buried in responsibility. Maybe you've forgotten how powerful your dreams really are.

Let this be your wake-up call. Because here's the truth: Your potential is not behind you. It's right here—in this moment, in your breath, in your next brave decision.

You were created with gifts this world needs. You carry wisdom no one else can offer. You are the only one who can live your dream. Don't wait for the perfect plan. Don't wait until you feel "ready." Don't wait for someone to rescue you from the noise of your own life. Start today. Write it down. Choose one dream. Take one step. Say yes to the you who is already becoming. You're not just someone with potential. *You are the dream.* And I can't wait to see what you build next.

One Bold Choice at a Time

You don't have to figure it all out today. You don't have to leap into a brand-new business model or burn your life down to build a new one. But you do have to choose. You have to choose to believe that your potential is still alive and still needed. You have to decide that your dreams are worth more than your doubts.

And you must take one bold step at a time. Prioritizing your potential isn't just beneficial for business; it's how you become the person you were always meant to be.

Meet the Author | Jean Tillery

Jean Tillery is a visionary leader and the driving force behind Epic Living with Jean, a platform dedicated to empowering individuals to lead their most fulfilling lives. A Certified Dream Manager, Jean combines her expertise in dream realization with her roles as the engaging host of the *#epicStories* podcast and inspiring a thriving community of dreamers and doers.

With a rich background as a home-schooling mom, Jean has honed skills in teaching, coaching, leadership, creation, and community building. Her journey is a testament to the transformative power of dreams. After years of envisioning a cross-country road trip—and overcoming significant physical and mental challenges, Jean embarked on the #epicRoadtrip, turning a long-held dream into reality. Today, she shares her powerful message about the importance of dreaming and living boldly.

Connect with Jean on her Facebook page, Epic Living with Jean, and visit her website at epiclivingwithjean.com. She would love to hear what living #epic looks like for you. Email her at jean@epiclivingwithjean.com.

It'll Be Different This Time

Ifedayo Greenway

I cannot believe I'm standing outside in a line that wraps completely around the building. It's pushing eighty degrees, I'm sweating through this long sweater that I had no business wearing, and I can't take it off because I'm definitely not dressed to be seen in public. I left the house thinking I'd knock out a quick errand and be back home before anyone I knew could spot me. All I wanted to do was handle my little piece of car business and go back home to get in bed, which is where I had planned to spend the weekend. I pulled up to the Department of Motor Vehicles (DMV) early on a Saturday morning, feeling accomplished like I'd outsmarted the weekend rush —only to find out I was already late to the party.

The line twisted around the building like we were waiting for a store to open with Black Friday deals. At first, I assumed we were just waiting for them to open; for business hours to start. Nope. Turns out they'd been open for almost forty-five minutes already, and it was *so* packed inside that the security guard had switched to a one-in, one-out policy just to keep the place from overflowing beyond capacity.

Folks behind me were going back to their cars to grab folding chairs and snacks like they had a whole picnic planned.

Me? I stood there unprepared, overheating, and completely blindsided by the mayhem. This was not how I planned to start my Saturday—caught up in early-morning DMV chaos and absolute buffoonery.

After being in that line for a little over an hour, every single thing started getting on my nerves—the pollen floating in the air like it had a personal vendetta, the bugs I had to keep fanning out of my sweaty face, the heat creeping under my sweater like it paid rent, and let's not forget the super whack dude standing directly behind me who kept trying to strike up a conversation. He said, "I'm not trying to holler at you" not once, not twice, but three times—sir, if you have to keep saying it, then chances are, you're trying to holla, and I'm not interested. *Uggh.*

I just wanted to press the restart button on my morning. I was one annoying moment away from saying, "You know what? Never mind," getting in my car, and abandoning the whole mission. I even started rehearsing what I'd tell the police if I got pulled over with expired tags. "Yes, officer, I *tried* to handle it, but the DMV line broke my spirit." As I inched closer to the front door, I started to feel a small flicker of hope. The frustration that had been sitting heavy on me started to loosen its grip. I'd done my best to tune everything out—the heat, the line, and the guy behind me. And now, for the first time all morning, I exhaled. I let myself be still, be present.

That's when I heard her.

A woman a few people behind me was on the phone, talking louder than most, but something about her voice cut through the noise. The world around me seemed to hush just enough for me to hear a phrase that hit me like a soft jolt: *"It'll be different this time."* I had no idea who the woman was talking to or what the conversation was about, but those five words—*It'll be different this time*—landed in my ear canals like they were meant for me. She could've been talking to a friend about a relationship, a job opportunity, or a second chance at something once lost. I'll never know the context. But she said it again. And then again. And somehow, those words echoed louder in my spirit than anything else I'd heard all day. *It'll be different this time* implies a hope or belief that a situation, often one that has previously gone wrong or been disappointing, will have a better outcome in the future. It suggests a shift in circumstances, mindset, behavior, or conditions that could lead to improvement or success this time around.

Maybe those words grabbed my attention because I was standing there in that line just thirty days into recovery from major surgery. My body was still healing, and so was my heart. I was still trying to make sense of what felt like a traumatic interruption—a moment with a scalpel that paused my life, stripped me of so much, and left me questioning everything. Would I fully heal? Would I ever feel like myself again? Could I find the strength to return to the entrepreneurial path I'd poured so much into? I felt emptied, physically weak, emotionally drained, and uncertain of my place in the world. There were days early on in my recovery where I genuinely considered giving up on it all. But that day, standing there in the heat and exhaustion, those five words—*It'll be different this time*—felt like more than a random phone conversation. They felt like a divine whisper, an answer to the quiet, desperate question I had asked God from my bed of affliction: *"Why should I even fight to heal and try again?"* And in that moment, it was as if He replied, gently and clearly: *"Because it'll be different this time.*

Earlier, I said that the phrase implies hope or belief in a situation, but the truth is, depending on the context, it can take on a few different tones. Those words can sound hopeful, full of fresh optimism—the kind that says, *"I've grown. I've learned. I've healed. And I believe this time will bring something better."* I've been there before. I've clung to that kind of hope when I was ready to believe in the possibility of something new, something redeemed. But they can also come from a place of naïveté or even denial—where the heart wants something so badly that it chooses to ignore the red flags, the familiar pain, the history that hasn't quite changed. I've spoken those words in that voice too (probably way too many times). Quietly, almost desperately, trying to convince myself that the past wouldn't repeat itself, even when the evidence suggested otherwise.

And then there's the determined, resolute tone—the voice that says, *"I've had enough. I'm showing up differently. I've changed my boundaries, my mindset, my strategy. I'm not just hoping this time will be different—I'm making it different."* I've stood in that version of the phrase, too, with grit in my soul and a fierceness in my eyes, choosing transformation even when it costs me everything comfortable. I imagine that her words hit so hard that day—because they echoed through me and touched every version of my voice that at one time or another in my life had embraced each of these tones. Standing there just fresh into recuperation, still nursing wounds—both seen and unseen—I chose to go with the tone that was deeply connected to the idea of potential—specifically, the belief that something or someone still holds untapped capacity for growth, success, or transformation despite past failures or setbacks. God used a stranger's conversation to remind me that my healing, my journey, my fight to move forward wasn't in vain.

By the time I reached this point in the chapter, I thought, *Whew! That's good. I've shared just about all I could share,* but then a question rose—quiet, persistent, and unwilling to be ignored. It tugged at my spirit, challenging me to dig deeper and expose the thoughts I hadn't yet put to paper: *Dayo, what exactly do you want to be different this time?*

The word *different* implies something not of the same kind—

something unlike what came before. Distinct. Set apart. Separate from the usual, the expected, the familiar.

In October 2024, I was diagnosed with a condition that I didn't know at the time, but would ultimately require surgery. That diagnosis came just two months after my youngest child and only daughter left for college in August, ushering me straight into the emotional whirlwind of empty-nest syndrome. After she left, I was quietly unraveling, trying to rediscover who I was and where I belonged. I had my first child at eighteen, so motherhood wasn't just a role—it was the bedrock of my adult identity. In a recent book I published, *A Piece of Change,* I wrote about the fears that surfaced when I entered this new chapter of life. I likened the empty-nest season to the transformation of a butterfly—vulnerable yet emerging. I asked the question, *"What are you afraid of, butterfly?"* And the honest answer? *"I'm frightened that this time, I will emerge from the cocoon as an unaccompanied, fragile, fluttering mess—my wings blanched and lacking the boldness of color I once carried as a parent."*

I ended that chapter with a vow to rise. To be reborn. To stretch my wings and fly, boldly and beautifully. But just two months later, I was thrust into a new, unexpected cocoon—one filled with medications that fogged my mind and drained my energy, a body that didn't cooperate, and a looming surgery that made me feel like maybe God was done with me. I started to wonder if my purpose had reached its expiration date. I had raised my children the best I knew how, and now they were out in the world, thriving. I had spent nearly a decade building a business as a transformational coach, pouring into women, helping them share their stories and own their change. While the business never quite took off in the way I dreamed, it had purpose. I had purpose. And now, all of that felt blurry. Distant. Faded.

The diagnosis—and the impending surgery—felt like a full stop. Like life was closing the curtain on chapters I hadn't even finished writing. Not in a way that made me want to end my life—no, that wasn't it.

But more like a resignation. A subtle acceptance that maybe my role had been fulfilled. Maybe I had given all I had to give.

So when I circle back to that question—*What do you want to be different this time?*—the answer is clear and raw and full of fire: I want to live. Not just breathe. Not just exist. Not just "make it through." I want to fly. I want to thrive. I want to feel the boldness of my color return. I want to reclaim the wings I once feared would fade. I want this new season—this post-surgery, post-empty nest, post-pause season—to be one of fullness, not finality. One of *revival*, not retreat. This time, I don't want to just survive the change—I want to be transformed by it.

How am I going to do that, you may ask?

Well, I used to tell my kids all the time, "When you know better, you do better." So here we are—at this moment in the writing, the reading, the *becoming*—and I have to tell both you and me: If we want different, we have to *do* different.

This is the moment where I say, *It's time to get up.*
No matter how many times you've hit what felt like the end...
No matter how lost or stuck you've felt...
No matter how exhausted you've been from trying and not seeing the results...
No matter how wounded you felt by the proverbial scalpels in your life...
No matter how traumatized you were by what happened—or didn't happen...
It's time to rise.
To move on.
To move *forward*.
To stop rehearsing the story of defeat and start prioritizing your potential.
To let faith in something new outrun fear of repeating the past.

You've got to put your hope in different—and act like it's already in motion.

Here are four steps to help guide you into that place of "different this time":

1. **Hope in Unseen Possibility**
    - Hope is more than a feeling—it's a mindset, a spiritual anchor, and a quiet rebellion against despair. It's choosing to believe that something better *can* happen, even when there is no evidence in sight to support that belief. That kind of hope takes guts and perseverance. It's not blind optimism; it's a decision to trust in what *could be*, not just what has been.
    - Sometimes, you have to hope with tears still drying on your cheeks. Sometimes, you'll hope while still cleaning up the wreckage of your last attempt. And yet, you speak life into a future you haven't seen because deep down you know your story isn't over. This kind of hope whispers, "Keep showing up" and demands your presence. It dares to envision wholeness while still walking through brokenness.
    - Hope in unseen possibility is what carried the woman with the issue of blood through a crowd to touch the hem of Jesus' garment. It's what helped Peter step out of the boat and onto the water. It's what lifts your eyes in the morning and tells your soul, "Try again." Even when you don't see it yet—even when the odds say otherwise —hope still stands.
2. **Faith in Change**
    - Change isn't just an option—it's a promise. Life itself is built on the rhythm of change: Seasons shift, tides rise and fall, and people evolve. But faith in change? That's personal. That's when you decide to stop anchoring

your future to past failures. It's when you believe that the same God who started a work in you is faithful to complete it.

- You are not stuck. You are not doomed to repeat every mistake. You are not bound to who you used to be. Faith in change is what allows you to speak over your own life, "I am not who I was—and I don't have to go back there." It invites you to imagine a life that aligns with your healing, not your hurt.

- Faith in change means refusing to let your past set the ceiling for your future. It's trusting that if you stay committed to growth, the change you seek will not only come—it will *stay*. It will embed itself into your mindset, your habits, and your heart. And eventually, the change you believed for will be the life you're living. Yes! Yes! Yes, change.

3. **Second Chances Rooted in Growth**

- Second chances aren't about doing the same thing twice —they're about doing it better because you've changed. The power of a second chance lies in who you've become since the first time. It's not about perfection. It's about perspective. It's about standing at the edge of an opportunity and saying, "I'm not the same person who fumbled this the last time."

- Growth turns regret into resolve. It teaches you to revisit old dreams with new wisdom and determination. What once felt like failure now becomes fuel. When you choose to grow, your second chance isn't a rerun—it's a reintroduction. And it's okay if the growth came through pain. Some of the most beautiful transformations are born from the darkest, most uncomfortable places.

- Second chances rooted in growth teach you to honor the process. You stop rushing toward results and start honoring the resilience you've built along the way. And when you do that, you step into a version of life you never thought possible—not because circumstances changed, but because *you* did.

4. **Risk and Vulnerability**

   o Believing *it'll be different this time* is a courageous act. It means cracking open your heart again after disappointment tried to lock it shut. It means trusting that just because something failed before doesn't mean it's destined to fail again. And that's a risk—not just emotionally, but spiritually and mentally. I know this one is not easy—even as I'm writing this, I'm learning to step out of my protective shell of isolation and gently lower the guardrails I've built around my heart.

   o Vulnerability is not weakness. It's strength dressed in softness. It's the ability to show up fully, even when you feel afraid. When you decide to believe again, dream again, try again—you're stepping out without guarantees. That's hard. But the greater risk is staying stuck in fear, living beneath your potential, and calling it safety.

   o Vulnerability is what allows love back in after heartbreak. It's what opens your mouth to speak again after silence. It's what moves your feet when they've felt frozen for far too long. And yes, there's a chance you might fall or get hurt again—but there's an even greater chance you'll fly.

   o Risk and vulnerability walk hand-in-hand with transformation. You cannot change without opening yourself to the unknown. But when you do, you make space for the miraculous. You give yourself permission to live again—whole, honest, and unafraid to want more.

Let this be your turning point.

Not because the path ahead is perfect—but because you are no longer pretending that you don't deserve different. Different requires intention. It doesn't just happen. It's a response to pain, a partnership with growth, and a bold declaration that your story is not finished. So if you're ready to rise, to rebuild, to reset and prioritize your potential, say it out loud with me: *It'll be different this time.*

Meet the Author | Ifedayo Greenway

Ifedayo Greenway is a mother, speaker, and master life coach. She is the chief executive officer of IG & MORE LLC. As a transformational coach, Ifedayo produces an annual event, The Change Experience, which empowers women to embrace the power of change in their lives.

She is the founder of the She Unveils movement where she serves and helps others accomplish their literary goals through unveiling, writing, and publishing their stories. She has been featured in *Huffington Post;* on CBS, FOX, NBC, and Shoutout Atlanta for her literary works (*Removing The Face* and *Removing The Fear*).

Ifedayo is a prolific author who has written nine books, five of which have been best-sellers. She holds the position of visionary author in four of those publications. Along with these books, she has also written inspirational articles that have reached thousands of readers through various mediums such as *Thrive Global* and *Faith Heart Magazine.*

Ifedayo Greenway

Ifedayo is passionate about her covenant with God to impact the world and uses her journey to strengthen and encourage women to find their authentic voice in their pursuit of transformation. Connect with Ifedayo at igandmore.com.

Sitting on Gold
Your Call is Waiting on You
Dr. Valarie Harris

Introduction

Your hidden potential isn't just a personal blessing in a world longing for hope, leadership, and solutions. It's a Kingdom assignment. Fear, uncertainty, and hesitation never intended to hide it away. They intended to prioritize, cultivate, and release it.

God has placed seeds of greatness inside us, gifts brimming with divine purpose and potential. Yet too many live their lives sitting on their gold, unaware of the hidden treasures. They wait for "someday" —someday when conditions are perfect, someday when they feel ready, and someday when fear loosens its grip.

But let me tell you, someday is not a day of the week.

Your potential isn't meant to remain buried. It's not meant to stay hidden beneath the fears, the doubts, or the distractions of life. It's meant to be unlocked, developed, and released. The world desperately needs leaders, healers, teachers, creators, and builders. And you have been equipped with a portion of the solution.

I am a living witness: When you prioritize your potential, you don't just change your life. You change lives around you. You unlock doors, heal hearts, build bridges, and leave a legacy that echoes through generations.

I believe with all my heart that you have the greatness the world needs inside of you. The question is, will you prioritize your potential and rise to the call?

Make no mistake: You are sitting on gold. And your calling can't wait.

Before I go deeper, let's define what prioritize and potential mean:

Prioritize (verb) means to designate or treat something as more important than other things; to arrange or deal with in order of importance.

Spiritually, prioritizing your potential means focusing intentionally on developing, stewarding, and activating the gifts and callings God has placed inside you rather than letting fear, distractions, or busyness take precedence.

Potential refers to the inherent ability or capacity for growth, development, or future success that has not yet been fully realized.

Spiritually, your potential is the God-given capacity He planted within you; gifts, talents, and divine assignments already residing inside you waiting to be recognized, nurtured, and unleashed.

Prioritizing your potential is an act of stewardship and obedience. It is your response to God's investment.

Biblical Foundation: God's Investment in You

Throughout Scripture, God makes it abundantly clear: We were created on purpose, for purpose.

Sitting on Gold

In 2 Timothy 1:6 (NIV), Paul exhorts his spiritual son Timothy: *"For this reason, I remind you to fan into flame the gift of God, which is in you..."*

In other words, don't let the gift sit idle; stir it up, feed it, and activate it.

Likewise, the Parable of the Talents in Matthew 25:14–30 reveals a powerful truth: God expects us to multiply our gifts, not let them stagnate. The servants who wisely stewarded their talents received praise. In contrast, the servant who buried his talent faced rebuke—not for doing evil, but for failing to act with what he had been given.

Jeremiah 1:5 (NIV) reminds us: *"Before I formed you in the womb, I knew you; before you were born, I set you apart."* Your potential is not random; it was planted in you before you took your first breath.

Ephesians 2:10 (NIV) declares: *"For we are God's handiwork, created in Christ Jesus to do good works, which God prepared in advance for us to do."* You were created for good works. But your potential must be prioritized and unlocked for those good works to manifest.

Finally, Proverbs 18:16 (NKJV) promises: *"A man's gift makes room for him and brings him before great men."* Your gift will open doors, but only if you steward it diligently.

Remember to prioritize your potential, as doing so demonstrates stewardship and obedience. God has already invested gifts, talents, and divine assignments within you.

Scriptures like 2 Timothy 1:6, Matthew 25, and Jeremiah 1:5 show us that our potential is real, intentional, and purposeful, but it must be recognized, developed, and multiplied.

Your potential is God's investment. Prioritizing it is your response.

Barriers That Can Block Your Potential

If our potential is so powerful, why do so many leave it dormant? The answer lies in a few common barriers:

- **Fear:** Fear of failure, judgment, and the unknown keeps gifts buried.
- **Procrastination:** "I'll do it later" becomes a lifetime of missed opportunities.
- **Lack of Clarity:** Even great potential can stay hidden without clear direction.
- **Comparison:** Measuring ourselves against others robs us of confidence and courage.

Yet 2 Timothy 1:7 (NKJV) reminds us: *"God has not given us a spirit of fear, but of power and of love and of a sound mind."* You have been fully equipped to overcome every barrier and prioritize what God placed inside you.

A Tool I Use for Prioritizing My Potential

Over the years, I've discovered that unlocking potential isn't accidental—it's intentional. I've built my life and business on the foundation of what I call the Seven Pillars of Transformation:

1. **Prayer**—Seeking divine clarity for the path forward.
2. **Passion**—Fueling the journey with what sets your heart on fire.
3. **Purpose**—Align your gifts with the Kingdom assignment uniquely given to you.
4. **Potential**—Recognizing and nurturing the greatness inside.
5. **Persistence**—Standing firm when obstacles try to derail your progress.

6. **Preparation**—Investing consistently in skill, wisdom, and spiritual depth.
7. **Positive Mindset**—Speaking life over yourself and your future daily.

These pillars are not optional in my life today. They are the framework for fully unlocking and prioritizing the potential God placed within me.

When You Prioritize Your Potential, the Real You Emerges

Did you know there is a version of you—the authentic, bold, radiant you—that only comes alive when you commit to unlocking your potential? The "real you" isn't the version weighed down by fear, self-doubt, or past failures. The real you is who God saw when He formed you: strong, courageous, impactful, and destined to shift atmospheres. When you prioritize your potential, several powerful things happen:

1. **You align with your divine identity.** Too many live beneath their spiritual identity, believing they are average, inadequate, or unworthy. But when you begin to steward your gifts intentionally, you start walking in your identity, not as someone trying to "become enough" but as someone who already is enough in Christ. Prioritizing your potential pulls you into alignment with who Heaven already says you are. You stop living based on your past or pain and start living based on purpose.
2. **You experience greater joy and fulfillment.** Joy isn't found in possessions or titles. It's found in purpose. When you operate from your unlocked potential, you experience the deep satisfaction of knowing you are fulfilling what you were born to do. Your days are no longer

about simply surviving—they become about impacting, building, sowing, and harvesting for God's glory. Jesus reminds us that joy is a byproduct of obedience and purpose. Prioritizing your potential unlocks that flow of supernatural joy.

3. **You shift from striving to flowing.** When you live disconnected from your God-given gifts, life feels like constant striving, forcing, pushing, and exhausting yourself without lasting fulfillment. But when you prioritize your potential, you move into divine flow.

- Opportunities start finding you.
- The right people are drawn to your light.
- Divine connections, resources, and open doors align because you are operating in your authentic assignment.

You don't have to manipulate outcomes. Your obedience becomes your advertisement.

Overcoming Limiting Beliefs About Your Potential

Even when we recognize our gold, limiting beliefs often whisper reasons why we should stay small. If you're going to unlock and prioritize your potential, you must dismantle these lies at the root. And I know this personally. At times, I struggled with limiting beliefs just like many others:

- Am I called to build more?
- Is there room for my voice?
- What if it's too late for me to step into a new level of leadership and impact?

The enemy tried to tell me that my season was finished, that others were better equipped, or that I had already "done enough." But God wouldn't let me settle. Through prayer, faith, and the Seven Pillars of Transformation I now teach, I had to break through those limiting beliefs and prioritize the deeper wells of potential God had placed in me.

And when I did?

- Doors opened.
- Impact multiplied.
- Joy returned.
- Legacy expanded.

Friend, I am living proof that when you confront and dismantle the lies about your potential, the real you emerges.

Most Common Lies and the Truths that Set Me Free

1. **I'm not good enough.**
   - **Truth:** You were never called because of your perfection; you were called because of God's purpose.
   - Second Corinthians 12:9 (NIV) reminds us: *"My grace is sufficient for you, for my power is made perfect in weakness."*
   - When I doubted my readiness, God reminded me: *"You don't have to be perfect, Valarie. You just have to be willing."*
2. **Other people are already doing it better.**
   - **Truth:** There may be many voices, but none carry your anointing, story, or unique mantle. You are not called to compete; you are called to complete. Isaiah 43:1 (NLT) says, *"I have called you by name; you are mine."*
   - When I looked around at others succeeding, I had to remind myself: No one can carry what God has assigned to my hands.

3. **This is a big one for me:** *"I missed my chance."*
   - **Truth:** Delay is not denial. God restores lost time. Joel 2:25 (NKJV) promises, *"I will restore to you the years that the locust has eaten…"*
   - When I thought it was too late to birth a bigger vision, God whispered, *"Daughter, I am the God who redeems time. Trust Me."*
4. "I don't know where to start."
   - **Truth:** You don't need to know the entire map—just the next faithful step. Psalm 119:105 (NIV) says, *"Your word is a lamp for my feet, a light on my path."*
   - God illuminated just enough for each step, revealing not the entire journey. I had to walk by faith, not sight, trusting that each new piece would emerge as I moved forward.

Keys to Shatter Limiting Beliefs

- **Renew your mind daily.** I soaked myself in Scripture, declarations, and faith-filled encouragement every day.
- **Speak life over your journey.** I declared God's promises aloud—even when my emotions tried to betray me.
- **Surround yourself with faith-filled voices.** I intentionally connected with mentors, coaches, and communities who spoke to my future, not just my past.
- **Take imperfect action.** I chose to act, even when I didn't have every answer.

Listen, the future you are dreaming of requires the real you to emerge. There's a *real* you the world has not seen yet—the bold, empowered, faith-filled, unstoppable you. Someone is waiting on the other side of your decision to prioritize your potential.

Today, choose to silence every limiting belief. Fan into flame every God-given gift. Step into the divine destiny Heaven has already declared over your life.

You are sitting on gold, and it's time to shine.

Sitting On My Gold

There was a time early in my journey when I didn't fully realize what God had entrusted to me. I was working hard, serving faithfully, yet there was a nudge inside my spirit—a restlessness that whispered, *"There's more inside of you."* At first, I brushed it off—after all, wasn't I doing enough? Wasn't I already making an impact? But deep down, I knew I was sitting on gold.

My passion for teaching, mentoring, and empowering others wasn't just a skill. It was a calling. It was not just any calling but a divine assignment to steward my potential intentionally, not accidentally.

I know what it feels like to be busy, successful on the outside, yet restless inside. I was serving, leading, and working, but there was that persistent whisper in my spirit: *"There is more inside of you."*

I realized that while using some of my gifts, I hadn't fully prioritized or stewarded the full measure of my potential. The divine whisper continued: *"There's more inside of you that you haven't even touched yet."*

In disobedience, I resisted. I rationalized, minimized, and distracted myself with busyness. But deep in my spirit, I knew I was sitting on gold.

It wasn't until I seriously applied the Seven Pillars of Transformation with new fire that I began to unlock the fullness of what God placed inside me:

- Through prayer, I sought divine strategy and not just my own good ideas.
- I reconnected with my passion—helping women unlock their hidden greatness.
- I aligned with my purpose—realizing it wasn't about "busyness" but impact.
- I nurtured my potential—investing time, resources, and faith to grow my gifts.
- I embraced persistence—even when doors closed or progress was slow.
- I am committed to preparation—studying, growing, and continually equipping myself.
- I guarded my positive mindset—speaking life over my destiny, even when circumstances said otherwise.

When I stopped sitting on gold and started stewarding it, doors opened; everything changed, and I started circulating it for the Kingdom. Lives were touched. Businesses were birthed. Legacies began to form.

Unlocking my potential unlocked my future and the future of those assigned to me.

How I Prioritize and Release My Potential

Unlocking your gold starts with intentional action. Here's how:

1. **Acknowledge the gold you're sitting on.** Take inventory of your strengths, passions, and experiences. Ask:
   - What do others often seek me out for?
   - What brings me joy when I do it, even without applause?
   - What burdens me to the point of action?

You can't prioritize what you don't recognize.

2. **Submit your potential to God.** Pray boldly: *"Father, awaken what You've planted in me. Teach me how to steward it with excellence and humility."*

3. **Clarify your assignment.** Potential without purpose is potential wasted. Ask:
   - Who am I called to serve?
   - What problem has God equipped me to solve?
   - What dreams keep resurfacing?
   - You are not called to everyone, but you are called to someone.

4. **Invest in your growth.** Prepare diligently through training, mentorship, study, and practice. A gift refined is a gift ready. You cannot fully unlock what you refuse to cultivate.
   - Take courses.
   - Seek mentorship.
   - Read, listen, and study to sharpen your gifts.
   - Practice boldly—even before you feel ready.

5. **Conquer fear with action.** Don't wait to feel fearless. Move forward despite fear. Courage is faith in motion.
   - Fear will always whisper, *"Who do you think you are?"*
   - Answer boldly, *"I am a child of God, carrying His assignment!"* When fear speaks, act anyway. Courage is faith in motion.

6. **Implement the Seven Pillars daily.** Transformation happens through daily intentional living, not one-time inspiration.

7. **Release your gold.** Potential is not meant to be hoarded; it is meant to bless others. Every time you show up, speak up, teach, lead, or serve, you are releasing Kingdom gold into the earth.

Don't wait for perfect conditions. Start now. Step out boldly. Sow into lives. Speak, serve, build, and lead—even when uncomfortable. Your release is someone else's breakthrough.

As I close, I know that your potential is needed now. You were created on purpose, for purpose, with purpose. The world doesn't just need another person living on autopilot. The world needs you fully alive, fully engaged, fully unlocked.

Don't die full.
Don't let fear, procrastination, or comparison rob you of your impact.
You are sitting on gold.
You were born with divine potential, and you were born for now.
The dreams you carry aren't random.
The gifts you possess aren't accidental.
You are a solution carrier, a legacy builder, a Kingdom advancer.
Friend, you are sitting on gold, and the world needs you to rise, unlock, and release it.
Don't let another year, season, or opportunity pass you by.
Prioritize what God placed inside you.
Multiply it. Steward it. Release it.
And now is the time to rise and release it.
The world is waiting.
Your calling can't wait. Your assignment can't wait.

Repeat this after me: "I have greatness inside of me that the world needs. I choose to unlock, prioritize, and release my God-given potential—for the glory of God and the good of those I am called to serve."

Prayer

Father, I thank You for the treasures You have placed inside me. Please give me the courage to unlock them, the wisdom to steward them, and the boldness to release them into the earth. Let me leave no gift buried and no assignment incomplete. Use me for Your glory, in Jesus' name. Amen.

Take some time to reflect and respond to these questions:

1. What gold (gifts, talents, passions) have I been sitting on?
2. What fears or barriers have prevented me from unlocking my potential?
3. Which of the Seven Pillars of Transformation do I need to strengthen the most right now?
4. Who are the people assigned to benefit from my unleashed potential?
5. What is one bold action I will take this week to prioritize and release my God-given gifts?

Remember this: The world is waiting on you.

Meet the Author | Dr. Valarie Harris

Dr. Valarie Harris, with an unwavering dedication spanning forty years of experience, has become a notable authority in education, leadership, and personal and professional development. Her perspective transcends geographical boundaries, exemplified by involvement with the mission's team for Global Missions in Ghana and India with endeavors that also extend to disaster relief efforts in Grenada, reflecting her unwavering dedication to humanitarian causes that uplift the underserved and vulnerable.

As an educator, minister, author, director of ministries, speaker, certified empowerment coach, and business consultant, Dr. Valarie leverages her expertise to empower leaders, educators, women, and aspiring entrepreneurs. Her teaching style fuses motivation, guidance, and empowerment, drawing from personal experiences to make content relatable and engaging.

She continues to inspire, encourage, and empower individuals to embrace growth and change and pursue their aspirations through her work and writings.

To learn more about Dr. Valarie, visit steppingoutwithpurpose.com or linktr.ee/talktimeval.

Pressing Through the Process

Lynn Lewis

I did not set out on a mission to become resilient. I was perfectly fine being a self-proclaimed encourager to women who I would meet along my way. On the night of August 4, 2019, my life took a sharp turn like one of those sharp curves in the road where if you glance back, the rear end of your car is still behind the curve and the front end is in front of it. It was the night I was informed that my son, Daniel Brooks Lewis, had been found deceased in another state, approximately five hours from where I resided. As the weight of grief settled in, resiliency was nowhere on my mind. I was simply trying to rationalize and make sense of the complicated, heartbreaking, gut-wrenching, unexplainable occurrence that had shown up in my life unexpectedly and most definitely uninvited.

Pressing through the process was what produced the resiliency necessary for me to get to the point of prioritizing my potential. In the beginning, I didn't even know the extent of my potential. In fact, it was not even on my mind during those first months after my son's death. I did come to know that I did not want to stay where I was in that broken place of despair. The grief was heavy. The ruminating always landed me back to where I started. Vacillating between reality and fantasy was a normal occurrence. In the fantasy, I did not have to believe what I knew was true.

It was seven months after Daniel's demise that I made a declaration to myself that while this tragedy would be a part of my life for the rest of my life, I was not going to allow it to consume me. As painful as it was to bear, I was determined not to die with my one and only child. I decided at that moment I was going to thrive in the aftermath of his death and not merely survive. I decided I was going to move forward with living an impactful, meaningful, and purposeful life. At the time I made the declaration, I did not know how, what it would look like, nor what it would entail, and I certainly had no thought or idea that purpose was wrapped up in my pain waiting to be revealed.

Each step forward, no matter how big or small, was preparing me for a version of myself I had not yet imagined—one anchored in faith, hope, and sheer determination. As I navigated my grief, I realized I didn't have to choose between grieving and growing. I could do both. This was a revelation that shifted everything. I gave myself permission to pause when needed, to cry without shame, and to laugh without guilt.

I invite you to come along with me as I share my journey of pressing through the process as a brokenhearted mother to a place of prioritizing my potential as a business owner. Also, consider this my personal invitation to you to honor your process, trust its unfolding, and embrace the strength that's being cultivated within you as you press forward. It's not a pretty, comfortable journey. It is one filled with highs and lows, ebbs and flows, disappointments, and regrets with some joy, peace, and happiness immersed throughout.

How did this process get started? As I mentioned earlier, I did not know what moving forward would look like. One day while perusing the World Wide Web, I found grief coaching. I did not know such a thing existed until that particular day. Further research revealed it was just what I needed. It would help me with my own healing process as well as afford me the opportunity to help others. I enrolled in the *From Grief to Gratitude Grief Coaching Certification Program* under the direction of Mrs. Dora Carpenter. By the time I completed the certification training, I knew I wanted to start my own grief coaching practice. I started Destined To Thrive Grief Coaching shortly thereafter. It felt like it would be a win-win situation. Not only would I benefit, but I would also be helping others do likewise as I was convinced that I was not the only griever who was choosing to move forward with life despite a devastating loss.

My son had been gone about two-and-a-half years by the time I completed the certification program in December 2021. I was feeling well and ready to help others as I continued to navigate my own grief. I had the tools. Unfortunately, I had the lived experience. I had the support of some peers and others. As life would have it though, there were more unexpected occurrences. One was my health challenges, which entailed four surgeries—two prior to the certification program and one each for the next two consecutive years. Aside from the health challenges, I reluctantly came to grips with the fact that I was not quite ready mentally nor emotionally to support others on their journeys, so I paused. My wholistic health and well-being became my priority. My focus shifted to practicing self-love unapologetically. Here is a side note: Do not fear a pause, a pivot, or a course correction. As you will see, I have had many while pressing through the process on my way to prioritizing my potential.

Once I came off pause, I found myself dabbling in a number of ways and strategies trying to figure this grief coaching thing out. As mentioned, I had the training, I had the tools and the support, but it just did not seem to be going anywhere. The one thing I did not do was give up. It's not that I didn't want to, but it's because I was certain and believed wholeheartedly that someone needed what I had to offer. I believed that what I had to offer was the solution to someone's problem or a life jacket that would keep someone afloat while they navigated their journey.

Lest I give up when I knew that was not what I was supposed to do, I gave myself some grace. I reminded myself that what I had endured over the past few years was indeed trauma. Not only was there the death of my son and the health challenges that resulted in numerous surgeries; there was also racial injustice and social unrest taking place at the same time. I did not shame myself when things did not go as planned, rather I adjusted, learned, and gave myself grace. It was all a part of practicing self-love.

I now know I needed those things to happen so I could move forward, to thrive and to experience joy, to live a meaningful and purposeful life in the face of adversity.

At the time of this writing, it's been almost six years since my son passed away. It's still a process, and I believe it will always be one. My grief has not gone away; I'm learning every day how to live with it. I actually don't want it to go away because it reminds me of my beloved child, that his life mattered and his memory is worth keeping alive. By now, you may be wondering how I got to the point of prioritizing my potential. I can tell you it was all about making a definitive choice to press through the process.

Let me tell you about the pressing. It was never by force; it was always a nudge in a forward direction. There were times I did not realize my position had changed until I took notice of where I was in comparison to where I had been. It often happened when someone brought it to my attention. I am so grateful for the people who believe in me, encourage me, and comfort me. I call them my pressers. It was during those times that I would think, *I really am moving forward despite the grief I have been burdened with.* As I'm writing this, I am reminded of a statement I read about the difference between the gap and the gain. The gap refers to how far we have to go; the gain refers to how far we've come.

Somewhere along the way, I began to recognize and own my strengths and weaknesses, take a closer look at some goals and habits, and with the help of some of my pressers, I noticed that transformation was taking place.

Do you remember earlier I talked about not being afraid of the pause, the pivot, or course correcting? Sometimes I don't want to acknowledge my strengths because my inner critic is pitting me against myself. I will succumb to what I perceive to be my weaknesses. Sometimes I get attached to the goals and habits that are no longer serving me well, if at all. This whole pressing through the process caused me to pause, quiet the inner critic, and course correct on some things. As a result, I considered my strengths and began to maximize them; I was no longer going to play small. I began to look at my weaknesses as opportunities to gain experience, revisited my goals and habits, and made changes accordingly.

There was the pause. Then the pivot happened as a result of me addressing some of my strengths, weaknesses, goals, and habits.

I discovered that one of my weaknesses was saying yes to anyone who had experienced a loss. I wanted to help everyone—no questions asked, I would say yes to it all. Well, I finally came to grips with the fact that I could not help everyone. I discovered that not everyone wanted or was ready for the guidance, help, and support I was offering. It became a reality that I was not the right coach for everyone nor was everyone the right client for me. Those were significant learning experiences for me and have been beneficial for maximizing my strengths.

More about the strengths later.

The initial goals I had set for my coaching services and the habits to support them were stagnant. Yes, I know goals and habits are not stationary; they should be reviewed and adjusted accordingly to be most effective. But I liked my goals and was determined to make them work. How did that work out for me? Not well. I ended up spinning my wheels and doing extraordinarily little other than shuffling papers and basically rewriting the same goals and sticking with the same habits that were not getting me anywhere.

Finally—yes, finally—course correction time.

I revisited why I started Destined To Thrive Grief Coaching, who I would serve, and how I would serve them. I started Destined To Thrive for the fifty-plus-year-old adult who had experienced the suicide death of a loved one. Despite it, they were ready to move forward with their lives but were in a *now what?* space and desired some guidance. I would support them by one-on-one coaching to help them move from pain to peace, heartbreak to happiness, and grief to gratitude with a plan specifically designed for their individual needs.

Now when I receive the calls, texts, and the like, I don't just say yes. I ask questions on the spot, or I invite people to schedule a complimentary chat with me to determine their needs and wants and if we are suited for each other as coach and client. When I come into contact with someone who is not suited for my services, I offer them resources that may better fit their needs.

There is some truth to the saying that old habits die hard—at least in my case. Once I began to loosen the grip on some of my habits that were not serving me well and revamp and set some new goals, I began to gain clarity. Goals were no longer only about achievement, but about meaning and impact. The one that comes to the forefront of my mind most often is being a guest on podcasts. Almost every time I saw an opportunity to be a guest, I took advantage of it. After being ghosted by hosts before or after recordings, the host doing far more talking than listening, and me doing two or three interviews a week, I learned some valuable lessons. Spending too much time in the grief space in a short span of time was emotionally toxic for me. I now only do two to three interviews a month. I also learned to vet the hosts prior to requesting or accepting an invitation to determine if I am their ideal guest.

Another thing that happened was I began to address the "you are so strong" comments when people addressed me as such. That was the result of a pivot, too. Moving forward, living an impactful, meaningful, and purposeful life is not synonymous with being strong. For me, it's always been making the choice to move regardless of how I felt—strong, weak, or somewhere in between. I now respond (when I deem a response is necessary) that it's not about how strong I am; it's about being resilient. I say resilient because for me, resilience is about adapting to circumstances, particularly those that I have no control over. My son's death was one such circumstance.

Transformation has taken place as I have pressed through grief. The process wasn't about getting over it; it was about learning to live with it as I moved forward. I continued speaking, sharing my journey, and coaching others who were also navigating grief as I had been doing while going through the pause. I discovered strength I never knew existed. The resiliency I experience today is the byproduct of the pressing—my capacity to love, to lead, and to lift others expanded. I am not defined by what happened to me, but by how I responded to it. It is a daily decision to embrace the transformation that has taken place in my life. I never dreamed I would know what turning one's pain into purpose was genuinely like; now I know. And because I know, I am determined to keep doing what I do because someone else needs to know, too. I may be the only conduit by which they come to know.

Each step forward pays homage to my declaration: I am going to thrive in the aftermath of my son's death rather than be consumed by it. I am not going to lose my mind, my joy, nor my peace.

The work I do now as a certified grief educator and coach is deeply personal. I get to support adults who find themselves in the *now what?* space after the death of a loved one; support them as they move from pain to peace, from heartbreak to happiness, and grief to gratitude on their own terms; help them rediscover their strength, rewrite their story, and reclaim their joy.

In doing this work, I honor my son. I keep his memory alive by helping others live more fully. I speak truth about grief. I remind others that healing is not about forgetting—it's about remembering with love and living with intention.

Prioritizing my potential was not a one-time decision, but a series of small, daily choices. I could sense that a shift was happening, but it wasn't until after it happened that I knew for sure. When I reflected on it, I knew it was because of the changes I made to my thought process, with my goals and the habits that supported them, and how I managed myself overall.

If you're experiencing a setback or feeling stuck while trying to prioritize your potential, I invite you to take a moment for yourself. Grab a notebook, journal, or electronic device; find a quiet space where you can be alone with your thoughts; and reflect on the list below. As you do, remember: Someone is waiting for you to show up. These are some of the key practices that have guided me along my journey:

- **Give yourself permission to pause.** Hit the pause button as often as you need. Use that time to reflect on your business, refresh your mindset, and adjust your goals accordingly. Course correction is not a sign of failure—it's an opportunity to do what is best for you and your business in the moment. I found it necessary to pause and pivot many times as I pressed through my own process. Review, rinse, and repeat as often as needed.
- **Embrace vulnerability.** If you do not know or understand something, ask. I encourage you to view

vulnerability as a strength instead of a weakness. As I've done this on my journey, it has been liberating.

- **Practice self-love unapologetically.** Self-love is not selfish—it is essential. It means protecting your health and well-being rather than sacrificing them for the sake of others. It is one of the most powerful gifts you can give yourself and those you serve. Be intentional about making yourself a priority on your calendar.

- **Network with purpose.** Networking is a powerful way to connect with potential clients, collaborators, and new opportunities. My suggestion is that you do not network just for the sake of it, but make sure it is purposeful. Be intentional and strategic to avoid burnout from going to meetings that may not be beneficial at that time—your time and energy are valuable.

- **Invest in your business wisely.** Financial investments in your business should be made with the long term in mind. Think about the potential for residual income or multiple streams of revenue that can grow from a single decision. A helpful tip: Prioritize investments that offer continued access to resources or materials even after the initial purchase.

- **Surround yourself with growth-minded individuals.** Connect with people who are heading in the direction you aspire to go—not to copy them, but to learn from their experiences. One of the greatest benefits I have found is being in community with others who are actively building their own businesses while teaching and inspiring others along the way.

- **Remember, social media is only a highlight reel.** What you see online is just a snapshot of someone's journey—not the full story. Do not let your inner critic convince you that you need to replicate everything you see. Pause and give yourself grace. Also, remind yourself it is okay to release that which is not serving you well. You never truly know what someone has overcome to reach their current level—unless they choose to share it.

I would be remiss if I didn't tell you that prioritizing my potential is an ongoing process, one that I am glad I embarked upon sometimes unknowingly. Yes, I get tired, weary, and worn, but I have no regrets. The strength and resiliency I have gained while navigating my grief journey and being able to truly turn my pain into purpose has been a phenomenal experience.

As I'm typing these last few sentences, please know that I'm thinking about you and hoping that my story has encouraged and inspired you to gift yourself with a plan to prioritize your potential, keeping in mind that it will produce resiliency, even in the face of adversity. Keep moving forward, but don't be afraid to glance back at your gain —to see just how far you have come.

Meet the Author | Lynn Lewis

Lynn Lewis is a certified grief educator, speaker, and author. She is also the visionary and chief empathy officer for Destined To Thrive Grief Coaching. Shortly after her son's tragic death in August 2019, Lynn made the choice to not be consumed by the grief of her loss.

She embraced the fact that she could not change what happened, but she could choose how she managed it. As a result, Lynn has turned her pain into purpose. She loves that she gets to support adults who are ready to move forward with living meaningful and impactful lives despite having experienced the loss of a loved one.

Lynn has been seen on NBC 12 and featured in publications such as *Richmond Free Press, Hope+Wellth,* and *GlamCEO.* She has also been a guest on podcasts such as *The Leftover Pieces, The Things We All Carry,* and *Heart 2 Heart with Keisha B.*

Connect with Lynn on her website (destinedtothrivegrief-coaching.com), Instagram (@griefcoachlynn) and on LinkedIn and Facebook.

Doing Your Due Diligence

A True Confession
Edwinette Moses

Am I the cause of my own lack of success?

How many times has this thought plagued us? We tell ourselves, *"I can do that,"* or *"If I were in charge, I would have done XYZ"* only to stop in our tracks, yielding to fear.

Fear of competition. Fear of expectations. Fear that we might have to live up to or produce what we are promoting.

The truth is, we all have something valuable to offer. But realizing that potential requires courage, discipline, and deliberate action—a commitment to doing your due diligence, not just in business or career, but in your own life.

Due diligence is about **ownership.** Ownership of your gifts. Ownership of your dreams. Ownership of your outcomes.

MaxPotential: Building a Foundation

A few years ago, my husband and I created a platform to encourage individuals of all ages to gain a foundational understanding of business and life concepts.

We held more than sixteen seminars, covering topics such as Personal Safety, Anatomy of a Credit Report, How to Purchase a Home, How to Purchase a Vehicle, Bankruptcy Basics, Credit Card Disputes, Wills and Trusts, and more.

When establishing the platform, we created an email address that included the phrase ***maxpotential.***

The theme was intentional: to help participants understand that within themselves was the potential for greatness—if they equipped themselves with the right tools and resources.

It wasn't about promising a perfect life.

It was about preparing people to handle the realities of life armed with wisdom, insight, and, most importantly, **due diligence.**

What Is Due Diligence?

In legal and financial terms, *due diligence* refers to a careful and detailed investigation or evaluation before entering into an agreement or taking an action.

In real estate, the *Residential Property Disclosure Act* emphasizes repeatedly: "The purchaser is advised to exercise whatever due diligence they deem necessary with respect to such information."

The message is clear: ***It is the purchaser's responsibility to investigate, to ask questions, to verify, to protect themselves.***

No one else can be held accountable for what you fail to discover.
And so it is with life.
You are the purchaser.
You are the investor.
You must perform your own due diligence before making decisions about your future.

Facing the Gap Between Comfort and Growth

As a Realtor, I have been fortunate to build my business through family, friends, and referrals. It has been a blessing—a foundation that provided stability and opportunity.

But if I am honest, it also allowed me to remain comfortable.

It kept me from pushing harder. From marketing myself boldly. From building a brand that would extend beyond my immediate circle.

Comfort was safe—but it was also ***stunting my growth.***

The hard truth is this: I delayed my own success by choosing comfort over intentional growth.

I confused being busy with being strategic.
I confused activity with advancement.
But now, it is time to move beyond convenience.
It is time to truly prioritize my potential.

A Lesson in Due Diligence: The Missed Walkthrough

Real estate has a way of teaching you life lessons you didn't know you needed.

One such moment came when I was representing a seller preparing a home for closing. After the inspection, several repairs were negotiated. The seller assured me everything was handled. Trusting the process—and honestly rushing to meet deadlines—I did not personally walk through the home with a checklist.

I assumed all was well.

On closing day, it was revealed that several agreed-upon repairs were incomplete.

The result? Delayed paperwork. Frustration for all parties. Strained trust. Extra stress that could have been avoided.

All it would have taken was a simple twenty-minute walkthrough with a checklist to verify the work.

Due diligence isn't about being suspicious. It's about being wise. It's about protecting the interests you are responsible for.

The Power of Doing Due Diligence: A Confident Buyer

On the flip side, I witnessed firsthand how powerful due diligence can be.

One buyer with extensive renovation experience purchased a fixer-upper. The inspection revealed multiple serious issues—the kind that would intimidate most buyers. But not him.

Due diligence didn't scare him.

It *empowered* him.

He knew exactly what he was buying because he had done his homework.

The flaws didn't deter him—they affirmed his confidence.

This is the *essence* of doing your due diligence in any area of life **—making informed decisions. Protecting yourself. Positioning yourself for success.** Preparation is power.

Tying It Together: Life, Law, and Learning

In every contract, real estate law advises, "The purchaser is advised to exercise whatever due diligence they deem necessary..."

That sentence echoes far beyond property transactions.

In life, **you are advised to exercise whatever due diligence is necessary** to protect your future, your dreams, your relationships, and your goals.

No one else will do it for you.
No one else is responsible for your readiness.
You must investigate.
You must prepare.
You must act.
Avoiding due diligence invites costly mistakes.
Performing due diligence builds confidence, credibility, and peace of mind.

I Am a Promise: Believing in Potential

As a child, the song *"I Am A Promise"* by Gloria and William Gaither left a deep impression on me:

> *I am a promise,*
> *I am a possibility,*
> *I am a promise with a capital P,*
> *I am a great big bundle of potentiality.*
> *And it continues:*
> *And I am learning to hear God's voice,*
> *And I am trying to make the right choices,*
> *I'm a promise to be anything He wants me to be.*

We are each **a promise.** We are each **a possibility.** We are each **a great big bundle of potentiality.**

But recognizing that potential isn't enough.

Prioritizing that potential—**doing the work** to steward it, grow it, and maximize it—is where the true journey begins.

You can have the seed of greatness inside you, but if you do not cultivate it, water it, protect it, and work it, it will wither and die.

Faith without action is dead.

Promise without due diligence is wasted.

Practical Steps: Building a Life of Due Diligence

Here are tangible ways to perform your due diligence in life:

- Study yourself: Identify your strengths, weaknesses, passions, and blind spots.
- Plan intentionally: Set clear, achievable goals with timelines.
- Prepare wisely: Research opportunities thoroughly before committing.
- Act boldly: Step forward, even when you feel fear.
- Review honestly: Periodically assess your progress and adjust as needed.
- Stay accountable: Surround yourself with mentors, advisors, and supporters who push you toward growth.

You are your greatest investment. Treat yourself accordingly.

Your Due-Diligence Challenge

If you take nothing else from this chapter, take this: ***Do your due diligence…on yourself.***

Study yourself. What are your natural strengths? Your interests? Your dreams? Where are your blind spots? What do you need to learn, improve, or overcome?

Don't just coast through life. Avoid mediocrity. Be intentional. Be strategic. Be honest. Be bold. You are a promise. You are a possibility. You are a great big bundle of potentiality.

But whether that potential is realized or wasted **is up to you.**

The Danger of Skipping Due Diligence

When we skip due diligence—whether in real estate, business, relationships, or personal development—we set ourselves up for disappointment and unnecessary setbacks. We assume things will work out simply because we *want* them to. We lean on hope instead of preparation.

Hope is a beautiful thing, but **hope is not a strategy**.

In real estate, skipping a home inspection can leave a buyer with expensive surprises: a leaking roof, bad plumbing, hidden termite damage. In life, skipping preparation can leave us stuck in jobs we hate, businesses that fail, relationships that hurt more than they heal, and dreams that die before they ever have a chance to live.

In the missed walkthrough situation I described earlier, I was not only representing my client, I was representing myself. I was building (or damaging) my reputation based on how seriously I took my responsibilities.

In fact, my signature line reads: *My people will live in peaceful dwellings, in secure homes, in undisturbed places of rest*—Isaiah 32:18 (NIV), a mantra is intended for both the seller and the buyer.

That experience burned itself into my mind: ***Always inspect what you expect.***

A simple checklist.
A short visit.
One extra phone call.
One more question.
Due diligence is often not difficult—it's just deliberate.

Choosing **not** to do due diligence may feel easier in the short term, but in the long term, it's far more costly.

Due Diligence and Dreams: The Hard Truth

It's easy to be excited when new opportunities present themselves. It's easy to talk about goals, ambitions, and dreams. But excitement without preparation is a trap.

You cannot wish your way into success. You cannot pray your way into success without also preparing, planning, and pursuing. Faith requires action. Dreams require work.

Due diligence is the bridge between desire and destiny.

Just like a wise homebuyer inspects every inch of the property before signing a contract, a wise dreamer inspects every part of the journey ahead:

- What skills will I need to develop?
- What sacrifices will I need to make?
- What obstacles are likely?
- Who can mentor or advise me along the way?

- What resources must I gather before I begin?

Every major step in life deserves this kind of thorough examination.

Comfort Is the Enemy of Growth

The most dangerous place to stay is not in failure—it's in comfort. Comfort tells you that good enough is good enough. Comfort tells you that stretching, growing, risking, and failing aren't necessary.

But nothing extraordinary ever grows in a comfort zone. I learned that the hard way in my real estate career. Working through friends, family, and referrals gave me a great start. but it didn't challenge me to expand. It didn't force me to sharpen my marketing, networking, communication, or negotiation skills. If I had remained content with only that small circle, I would have capped my own potential.

Stretching Beyond Safe Spaces

Today, I see that doing my due diligence isn't just about inspecting properties or reviewing contracts. It's about inspecting *my own effort, my own mindset*, and *my own actions*.

Am I truly putting in the effort to market my business with excellence? Am I strategically reaching out to potential clients outside my comfort circle? Am I investing in ongoing education to stay competitive and sharp? Am I building relationships that stretch me and position me for bigger opportunities?

When we conduct due diligence on our dreams, we realize how much power we actually have. We realize that the barriers holding us back are often self-imposed.

Fear.
Procrastination.
Self-doubt.
Laziness.
Distraction.

But just like a homebuyer has the right to walk away from a bad deal, we have the right to walk away from bad habits and limiting beliefs.

Due diligence gives you choices.

When you gather information, you gain power. When you evaluate risks, you reduce anxiety. When you prepare wisely, you walk boldly.

Due diligence is an act of self-respect. It is an act of self-investment.

Preparing for the Next Level

Preparation doesn't mean waiting until everything is perfect. Preparation means building a foundation sturdy enough to carry the weight of your dreams.

There will always be unknowns. There will always be risks. There will always be moments when you must step out in faith.

But when you have done your due diligence—when you have prepared mentally, spiritually, emotionally, financially—you will be able to withstand the storms that come.

I had to learn this both as a realtor and as a person prioritizing my potential.

When my business was fueled solely by friends and family, I didn't need much infrastructure. I didn't need strong marketing systems, clear client processes, or scalable growth plans. But to grow—really grow—I needed to think differently. I needed to stop treating my calling like a casual hobby. I needed to start treating it like a serious, thriving business that deserved my best.

The same is true for any dream you hold dear.

Due diligence is not just about **protecting** what you have—it's about **preparing** for what's next.

The Promise Inside You

The lyrics of *"I Am A Promise"* come back to me often when I think about potential:

> *I am a promise,*
> *I am a possibility,*
> *I am a promise with a capital P,*
> *I am a great big bundle of potentiality.*
> *And even more powerfully:*
> *I am learning to hear God's voice,*
> *And I am trying to make the right choices,*
> *I'm a promise to be anything He wants me to be.*

These words remind me that promise alone is not enough.

A seed is full of promise, but if it is never planted, watered, and nurtured, it will never become a tree. It will never bear fruit. It will never fulfill its potential.

We are the same.

Our potential must be prioritized, protected, and pursued with intentionality.

Otherwise, it lies dormant—wasted.

You were never meant to simply exist. You were never meant to coast. You were never meant to settle.

You are a promise. You are a possibility. You are a great big bundle of potentiality.

But the realization of that promise is tied directly to your willingness to do your due diligence—on your skills, your opportunities, your dreams, and your destiny.

Faith Without Action: The Missing Link

Hearing God's voice and trying to make the right choices as the song *"I Am A Promise"* beautifully says is essential, but it requires more than just hearing. It requires doing.

Faith is powerful.

Belief is beautiful.

But without corresponding action, even the strongest faith can wither. I realized that for too long, I had believed in my promise, my possibility, my potentiality, but I wasn't *moving* in it consistently. I allowed comfort to numb my urgency. I allowed procrastination to delay my obedience. I allowed fear to slow my progress.

Hearing God's voice is only the beginning.

Due diligence in life means **following through**, even when you are scared, even when success feels unfamiliar, even when no one else claps for you.

Faith calls us to action. Potential calls us to preparation. The promise inside us demands a response. If we are willing to work—to sow, to invest, to prepare—the fruits of our labor will come. But the choice is ours.

Checklist for Prioritizing Your Potential

If you're serious about maximizing your strengths, achieving your goals, and transforming your life, here's a simple **due-diligence checklist** you can start using today:

Study yourself. Spend time reflecting on your skills, passions, limitations, and blind spots. Write them down. Get to know *you*.

Set specific goals. Dreams without deadlines are just wishes. Break your dreams into tangible, time-bound goals.

Prepare for obstacles. Identify what challenges you might face. Prepare strategies to overcome them ahead of time.

Find mentors and accountability partners. Who is already doing what you dream of doing? Seek their wisdom. Stay accountable.

Invest in yourself. Whether it's reading books, taking courses, networking, or practicing your craft, continually invest in personal growth.

Inspect your progress regularly. Every thirty days, take stock. What's working? What's not? Adjust without losing momentum.

Celebrate milestones. Progress deserves celebration. Recognize and honor how far you've come, even as you continue moving forward.

Stay teachable. Success can make people complacent. Stay humble. Stay teachable.

Sample Due Diligence Action Plan

Sometimes, we hear inspiring advice but wonder, *What does that actually look like?*

Here's a simple **action plan** I've created based on my journey right now. You can use the same concept to create your personalized plan as well.

Goal: Grow my business beyond friends and family referrals.

Due-Diligence Steps:

- Research three new marketing methods this week.
- Create a social media presence (or enhance existing one).
- Attend one networking event in the next thirty days.
- Schedule a twenty-minute meeting with a successful peer to ask for advice.
- Read one book or listen to one podcast about scaling a service-based business.
- Create a simple tracking sheet for outreach, follow-ups, and appointments.

Goal: Prepare for a career pivot or promotion.

Due-Diligence Steps:

- Update your résumé and LinkedIn profile by the end of the month.
- Identify and register for one relevant certification or continuing education opportunity.
- Conduct three informational interviews with people in your desired field.
- Volunteer for a leadership opportunity at work to gain new experience.
- Create a six-month personal development plan with measurable targets.

Goal: Strengthen my faith walk and spiritual growth.

Due-Diligence Steps:

- Commit to a daily devotion and prayer time, even if only ten minutes a day.
- Memorize two Bible verses a month related to purpose and perseverance.
- Find a small group or accountability partner.
- Identify and eliminate one major distraction preventing deeper growth.
- Serve once a month in a ministry that stretches you beyond your comfort zone.

Final Reflection: Your New Beginning

Doing your due diligence isn't just a wise career move. It's not just about business, contracts, or real estate deals. It's a **way of life**. It's a decision to no longer live passively. It's a commitment to no longer accept mediocrity. It's a covenant with yourself to honor the gifts, talents, and dreams that God placed inside you.

When I look back on the missed opportunities, the moments where fear spoke louder than faith, I feel no shame, only gratitude that I now see the truth more clearly.

You are not too late. You are not too far behind. You are not too broken. The promise inside you is still alive. The possibility is still real, but now is the time to act. Now is the time to build. Now is the time to believe boldly—and to move with wisdom and strategy.

You are a promise. You are a possibility. You are a great big bundle of potentiality. And with God's guidance, your own faith, and your own daily due diligence, you can and will become everything you were created to be. The next chapter of your story begins with the steps you take today. ***Step forward. Step wisely. Step boldly.***

The world is waiting for the full, flourishing, fearless version of you.

Meet the Author | Edwinette Moses

Edwinette Moses has an extensive career with the Department of Veterans Affairs, Veterans Health Administration (VHA), with more than twenty years of service. During her tenure, she has received five promotions in leadership capacities and currently serves as an administrative officer/executive assistant in the National Radiation Oncology Program Office, which provides oversight of VHA Radiation Oncology Services nationwide. Additionally, she manages several multi-million-dollar contracts on behalf of the program office.

Edwinette is an entrepreneur and has several business ventures to include a family business, Second Look Flea Mart, which launched in 2010. This business has two models—the brick-and-mortar operation is one-day-a-week and an online store.

Edwinette is a licensed Realtor with experience in both residential and commercial sales and residential property investing for several years.

Early entrepreneurship began with a medical billing and coding consulting service with a focus on reimbursement services.

Edwinette holds a bachelor of arts in liberal arts with a focus on independent studies from the University of Richmond, as well as a certification as a health records coding technician from J.S. Reynolds Community College.

She is a charter member of the Central Virginia Chapter of Top Ladies of Distinction, Inc.®, supports various community service programs and projects.

She has been married for more than 36 years and has one daughter and one granddaughter. Edwinette likes spending time with her family, enjoys shopping and a little bit of traveling.

Contact her via email at emoses@gohtr.com or follow her on Facebook at Edwinette Moses, Realtor.

Wholistically Piecing Your Purpose
Anchoring Your Life in Mind, Body, and Spirit
Dana Wilson

S ome decisions don't just shape your life—they crack you open first. They tear through your plans, stretch your faith, and demand a new kind of courage.

I didn't know it then, but I was standing at one of those crossroads—the kind you can't prepare for; the kind that splits your heart wide open.

At the time, my son Landon's care needs were increasing. His medical condition required multiple therapies, frequent appointments, and round-the-clock attention. I was constantly navigating doctors, specialists, and the unknowns of developmental delays. The thought of being absent during those formative years—missing critical milestones or not being there when he needed me most—made my chest tighten.

I didn't just *want* to be there full time. I *needed* to be. I was his primary advocate, his interpreter, his lifeline. And the more the military asked me to show up everywhere else, the more I felt I was failing where it mattered most—at home.

I was weighing the decision to abruptly leave the military so I could be with my son full time, with no financial plan and only my emotions leading the way.

My heart said *stay with him,* but everything else—the bills, the benefits, the unknown—screamed for a safety net.

And then came Ms. B.

We spent nearly two weeks together, and looking back, I know that time was divine. Ms. B was eighty years old, steady, observant, and overflowing with the kind of wisdom you don't find in books. She didn't come to fix me—she came to *center* me.

One afternoon, as I sat emotionally undone, she looked me in the eyes and said gently, *"Dana, I live on a fixed income. No side hustle. No extra checks. Just senior discounts, coupons, and blessings, and I make it."*

She continued, *"Retiring from the military won't make you rich, but it will offer you something more important—stability, structure, and the medical care your son will need. Five years may feel like forever to you now, but when you're my age, it's a blink, especially with a child whose future needs you haven't even seen yet."*

She was right. Every word wrapped itself around my anxiety like a blanket. It didn't erase the fear, but it reframed the future. She gave me permission to zoom out and consider the long game—for me and my son.

I had been ordered to a new assignment in California, and while the military technically had the resources to support Landon, it was determined that the continuity of his care—the trusted doctors, therapy providers, and routines in Virginia—would be best left undisturbed.

That decision shattered me. I didn't want to leave him behind, even temporarily. But at the time, I had no clear path forward, and no authority to override what others deemed "best."

So I reported for duty in California—without my son.

That decision broke something open in me. I moved forward physically, but emotionally, I unraveled. The weight of separation, the ache of uncertainty, and the question that wouldn't leave me alone: How could this possibly be the life I was meant to live?

Everything looked functional on the surface, but my soul was screaming. I was showing up for duty, checking every box, but I felt like I was living outside of my own body.

In the military, separation from your children is standard. Deployments, distance, logistics—it's all part of the job description. Most people just accept it. But I couldn't. Not in my mind. Not in my body. Not in my spirit.

When the court denied my petition to bring Landon with me due to his medical needs, it felt like someone had snatched the air from my lungs. I couldn't sleep. I couldn't think. I was showing up in uniform, but inside, I was falling apart.

I began to question everything. Was I walking in purpose or just walking in circles? The vision I'd always held for my life—of being a present, powerful mother and a purpose-driven woman—felt like it was slipping through my fingers.

But somewhere deep within the chaos, a seed of new thinking started to sprout. What if my purpose wasn't unraveling—what if it was being reassembled? It wasn't easy, and it wasn't instant. But it was the beginning of a shift: from surviving the separation to seeing a bigger divine strategy at play.

Mind: The Mental Puzzle of Purpose

Maybe you've had a season like that too—a season when your mind felt like a battlefield instead of a blessing. Where the louder voices told you to give up, to settle, to play it safe—while somewhere deep within, a quieter whisper urged you to believe in something you couldn't yet see.

If you find yourself standing between what was and what could be, I invite you to pause and ask yourself:

- What stories have I been telling myself about my life, my worth, my future?
- Are these stories rooted in fear or in possibility?
- What if the confusion I'm experiencing is not a sign of failure, but a sign that my old mindset is making room for something greater?

Your mind is not your enemy. It is the soil where new purpose can take root—if you are willing to plant new thoughts and nourish new beliefs.

Not long after settling into California—going through the motions of a life that didn't feel like mine—something unexpected happened.

I received an email about an early retirement opportunity being offered to only a small, select group. The eligibility requirements were strict—almost razor-thin. You needed to have completed at least fifteen years, but less than sixteen years of service. You needed one full year on station.

I read those requirements again and again, hardly believing my eyes.

I had fifteen years, eleven months, and twenty-six days of service—four days short of sixteen years.

I was stunned.

I couldn't have scripted the timing if I tried. It felt too precise, too exact to be random. It was like a whisper from heaven saying, *"I see you."*

There was just one obstacle: I hadn't been stationed in California for a full year yet—only a few months. Without hesitation, I ran to my commander and requested a waiver. I knew I had to try.

We sat down for a candid conversation. I explained that I couldn't ignore the door that had cracked open, even if it seemed improbable. He listened. He warned me not to get my hopes too high—that waivers weren't guaranteed, and disappointment was likely.

Still, he signed off.

I submitted my application for early retirement and entered a season of waiting.

While I waited, life didn't slow down. In fact, it sped up. I was immediately pulled into deployment preparations—intense exercises simulating war, donning gas masks, crawling through fields with loaded rucksacks, rehearsing accountability protocols, living every day as if a real deployment order could come at any moment.

I remember the last day of a grueling field exercise. I came home physically battered, mentally drained, and spiritually weary. Every part of me—mind, body, and spirit—was stretched thin.

I dropped my gear by the door, sank onto the floor, and checked my email, not expecting anything, and there it was.

My approval letter.

The waiver had been approved as well—both answers tucked into that single, life-altering message.

My fifteen years, eleven months, and twenty-six days of service—just shy of sixteen years—had been accepted for early retirement.

I dropped to my knees right there in my living room. Tears streamed down my face. I wasn't alone. I hadn't been forgotten. God had me— He had me the entire time, even when I couldn't see it. Even when it felt like everything was falling apart.

That moment wasn't just about leaving the military. It was about stepping into a new kind of service—the kind rooted in purpose, wholeness, and full surrender.

Within just a few months, I was physically reunited with my son.

The moment I wrapped my arms around him, I knew deep in my bones that my instincts had been right all along. I was never meant to live separated from him. Being without my son was never aligned with my true purpose.

I became fully convinced that it was my obedience—not my striving —that opened the door. God had sent me to California, not to abandon me, but to position me—to retire me early, to secure the benefits and stability that my son and I would need for the journey ahead.

For the first time in a long while, my mind, my body, and my spirit were at peace.

Now, I had another mission ahead of me.

How was I going to financially take care of us while having the flexibility to attend to my son's many doctor visits, therapy appointments, and daily care needs?

I went to my treasure chest—the place where my skills, knowledge, and lived experiences were tucked away, waiting for this exact moment.

And when I opened it, I pulled out something that had always been there: my love for hair care, my understanding of beauty, and my gift for healing hands.

I stepped into full-time hair care entrepreneurship.

This path allowed me to do something the military never could: dictate my own schedule, regulate my income, and most importantly, be fully present for my son.

I wasn't just building a business.

I was piecing together a new life.

Body: Listening to the Physical Signs

My body had carried so much for so long—more than I had ever given it credit for.

Years of military service had taught me how to push past exhaustion, to perform through pain, to keep going even when every fiber of my being screamed for rest. I had worn resilience like armor, believing that strength meant ignoring my body's quiet cries for care.

But now, with my son back in my arms, my time my own, and a new path unfolding before me, I couldn't ignore it anymore. My body was tired. Tired in a way that sleep couldn't fix.

I realized that freedom wasn't just about controlling my schedule—it was about reclaiming my health.

The tightness in my chest, the tension in my shoulders, the thinning of my hair—all of it had been messages my body was sending me, long before I had the space or the courage to listen.

Stepping into entrepreneurship gave me more than a flexible calendar. It gave me permission to slow down, to nourish myself, to restore what had been depleted.

I started paying attention to the signs: what foods fueled me and what drained me, what movement energized me and what wore me out, how my body responded to peace versus pressure.

Our bodies are storytellers, too.

Long before the mind admits fatigue, the body has been whispering—sometimes shouting—for us to listen.

If you pause right now, what is your body trying to tell you?

- Where does tension live in your frame?
- What physical signs have you been ignoring, dismissing, or minimizing?
- How would your life change if you treated your body not as a machine, but as a miracle?

Freedom is not just found in flexible schedules or career wins—it's found in honoring the sacred vessel that carries your purpose forward.

For the first time in years, I wasn't fighting my body. I was learning to partner with it.

Because piecing together my purpose meant honoring every piece of me—and that included the vessel carrying me through it all.

Spirit: Fueling Purpose from Within

Healing my mind gave me clarity. Healing my body gave me energy.

But it was my spirit that gave me life.

For so long, I had been surviving on grit alone—pushing past emotions, soldiering through circumstances, doing whatever it took to "make it."

But obedience—answering the call to California, enduring the season of separation, trusting what didn't make sense—had taught me something that grit alone never could: Purpose doesn't flow from striving. Purpose flows from surrender.

I realized my spirit hadn't been broken during those hard years. It had been forged.

Every tear, every unanswered prayer, every lonely night was not a punishment—it was preparation.

I wasn't being forgotten. I was being fortified.

The more I honored my spirit—through prayer, stillness, worship, reflection—the stronger I became. Not the kind of strength that puffs up and powers through, but the kind of strength that moves with certainty and peace, even when the next step is unclear.

My spirit began to lead, not just my healing—but my decisions.

I chose clients based on alignment, not desperation. I said yes to opportunities that felt life-giving and no to ones that drained my peace. I built my business, my family life, and my personal growth strategy around a simple question: Does this honor the woman God is calling me to become?

There is a strength that only spirit can give—the kind that sustains you when strategies fail, when plans collapse, when human effort is not enough.

As you reflect on your own journey, consider:

- When was the last time you fed your spirit—not just your schedule?
- What daily practices reconnect you to the deepest part of yourself?
- Where in your life are you relying on grit when your spirit is asking for grace?

Your spirit is not asking for perfection. It is asking for presence—for you to come back home to yourself, over and over, until wholeness is no longer a wish but a way of life.

When I started leading from my spirit—not just my mind, not just my body—my entire life shifted.

I wasn't just piecing together a career. I was piecing together a calling.

Empowering You: Piecing Together Your Own Purpose

If you see yourself somewhere in my story—standing at a crossroads, carrying more than you feel capable of holding—I want you to know: You are not broken. You are becoming.

Your mind may feel cluttered with questions. Your body may be tired from battles no one else can see. Your spirit may be weary from carrying silent hopes for so long.

But hear me: Your purpose is not lost.

It's waiting for you to piece it together—wholistically, intentionally, and without apology.

Every experience you've endured, every lesson you've learned, every moment that tried to break you has actually been shaping you.

Your mind matters.

Your body matters.

Your spirit matters.

Start where you are. Listen to your mind with compassion. Tend to your body with care. Feed your spirit with truth.

You don't have to have it all figured out.

You don't have to piece it all together overnight.

You just have to believe that wholeness is possible—and worth it.

Wholistically Piecing Your Purpose

I am living proof that even the most broken seasons can lead to the most beautiful purposes.

And if I can piece my purpose together—mind, body, and spirit—so can you.

Every strand counts.

Every step matters.

Every piece belongs.

With love and purpose,
Dana

Meet the Author | Dana Wilson

Dana Wilson is a certified trichologist, Sisterlocks™ consultant, empowerment coach, and the CEO and director of Hair Cares Inc. A retired Air Force veteran and devoted mother, she empowers women to piece their lives together wholistically—mind, body, and spirit—through beauty, business, and purpose. Dana believes that every root, every lesson, every experience, and every legacy makes a difference in our lives.

Through her signature framework, *The 10 Keys to a Wholistic Approach to Hair Growth,* Dana blends science, spirituality, and self-care into a transformational path that empowers women to take control of their health and their beauty. Her work bridges beauty and wellness, helping clients piece together their purpose—mind, body, and spirit.

She believes that every strand counts—every root, every lesson, every experience, and every legacy makes a difference in our lives.

Maximize Your Strengths, Achieve Your Goals, Transform Your Life

Kathleen Kim Moore

Introduction: The Call to Potential

*P*otential is a word that stirs something deep within me. It's more than an idea; it's a divine seed, rich with promise and power, waiting for the right soil and season to blossom. I've always believed that within each of us lies untapped brilliance—a vision, a ministry, or a business that reflects our God-given purpose.

For me, unlocking that potential in others has become more than just a calling—it's my life's work.

I am Pastor Kathleen, the founder and visionary behind Living The Dream Consultants LLC. With more than four decades of experience in administrative leadership across government, healthcare, banking, and technology, my journey has been anything but linear. It's been a tapestry of faith, discipline, and strategic decisions. But it wasn't until I stepped out in obedience to establish my business that I truly saw the fullness of what it meant to prioritize potential—not just in others, but also within myself.

Living The Dream Consultants LLC is more than a business name. It is a prophetic declaration. Every strategy developed, every document prepared, every ministry or business assisted—it all speaks to the belief that when we structure our vision with intention, we give it the opportunity to thrive.

In this anthology, I want to walk you through what it looks like to honor the dreams God gives us by stewarding them well. My hope is that as you read, you'll be inspired to recognize your potential, prioritize your process, and walk boldly in purpose, knowing that you too can live the dream.

From Vision to Venture: Building on a God-Given Blueprint

The vision for Living The Dream Consultants LLC didn't appear out of thin air—it was birthed through prayer, fasting, and years of cultivating administrative excellence within other people's visions. I served faithfully in ministry and corporate spaces, sharpening my skills, strengthening my resolve, and recognizing patterns in what made organizations thrive—or fail.

It became clear to me that many people had powerful visions but lacked the infrastructure to support them. They had passion but lacked planning. They had calling but lacked systems. That's where God called me to step in—not just as a consultant, but as a vessel of clarity, order, and divine alignment.

Living The Dream was not about chasing a career, it was about walking in purpose.

The transition from vision to venture required courage. I had to trust that the same God who gave me this dream would also provide the resources, connections, and clients. I started with what was in my hands: decades of experience, a deep network, and a passion for systems that support sustainability.

My first clients were ministries that had dreams but needed help bringing them into compliance and structure. They needed bylaws, 501(c)(3) documentation, licensing, board development, and strategic planning. I realized that this wasn't just administrative work—it was apostolic in nature. I was helping lay the foundation for Kingdom work to be done in decency and order.

The vision became a venture because I treated it with the seriousness and stewardship it required. I invested in certifications, continued my education, and surrounded myself with trusted advisors. That venture—once just a whisper in prayer—is now a thriving consultancy supporting leaders nationwide.

Strategic Execution with Spiritual Excellence

One of the major lessons I learned early is this: Anointing needs administration. Purpose without a plan leads to frustration.

Key Areas for Training Top-Notch Administrative Staff

Professional Communication Skills: Emphasize clear, courteous, and professional verbal and written communication for emails, phone calls, meetings, and public interactions.

Calendar and Schedule Management: Train staff to expertly manage complex calendars, schedule meetings, avoid conflicts, prioritize tasks, and anticipate executive needs.

Document Management and Recordkeeping: Teach best practices for organizing digital and physical files, handling confidential information, and maintaining proper documentation.

Meeting and Event Coordination: Train on planning logistics for meetings, conferences, and offsite events, including agendas, minutes, room setups, catering, and technology needs.

Technology Proficiency: Ensure fluency in Microsoft Office Suite, Google Workspace, Zoom, project management software (like Asana or Trello), and CRM [Customer Relationship Management] tools.

Financial and Budget Administration: Provide training on managing invoicing, expense reporting, petty cash, purchase orders, and basic budgeting processes.

Critical Thinking and Problem-Solving: Develop the ability to anticipate needs, resolve conflicts quickly, troubleshoot challenges, and make sound decisions independently.

Customer Service Excellence: Train staff to create a positive first impression, handle difficult situations gracefully, and deliver consistent, high-quality service to internal and external stakeholders.

Time Management and Prioritization: Teach how to juggle multiple responsibilities, set realistic deadlines, maintain productivity, and focus on high-impact tasks.

Professionalism and Workplace Etiquette: Cover expectations for personal presentation, ethical behavior, confidentiality, diplomacy, and relationship management with all levels of leadership.

At Living The Dream Consultants LLC, strategic planning is the foundation. Every engagement starts with clarity:

- What is your vision?
- Who are you called to serve?
- What resources are needed?
- What systems must be built?

I teach my clients to map their visions using what I call the Blueprint for Success. This includes:

- Vision Statements
- Strategic Goals
- Milestones
- Administrative Systems
- Financial Accountability
- Growth Plans

I remind every leader and entrepreneur: "It is not enough to be passionate. You must also be prepared."

The same diligence we bring to corporate environments should be reflected in our ministries and businesses. Preparation is a form of worship. Excellence honors God.

I have walked alongside ministries that started in living rooms and now own multiple acres. I have consulted businesses that moved from concept to six-figure revenues. It's not magic—it's strategic stewardship.

And at the core of it all is the principle of faithful execution.

Tips for Consulting Small Business Startups

Clarify the vision and mission early. Help clients articulate a clear business vision and mission. Everything—from operations to marketing—should align with this foundation.

Focus on legal and structural setup. Guide them through choosing the right business structure (LLC, corporation, et cetera), registering the business name, obtaining an Employer Identification Number (EIN), and securing necessary licenses.

Create a basic, actionable business plan. Encourage a simple but focused business plan that outlines objectives, target markets, products/services, revenue models, and a timeline for execution.

Prioritize financial planning and budgeting. Stress the importance of setting up a business bank account, simple bookkeeping systems, understanding startup costs, and planning for six to twelve months of operations.

Emphasize the power of branding. Assist in developing a basic brand identity—logo, tagline, brand colors—and a clear brand voice that reflects their business values.

Simplify the launch strategy. Recommend starting with a Minimum Viable Product (MVP) or a soft launch to test the market before investing heavily.

Teach smart time and task management. Introduce basic project management tools (like Trello, Asana, or Monday.com) and calendar discipline to help them stay organized.

Encourage building an online presence early. Recommend a professional website, a business email address, and consistent social media profiles. Basic search engine optimization and Google Business registration are crucial.

Stress networking and relationship building. Teach them that early partnerships, community involvement, and referral networks can often drive their first major wins.

Prepare for resilience and adaptability. Help them expect obstacles and encourage a mindset of continuous learning, pivoting when necessary, and staying flexible without losing the core mission.

Event-Planning Tips

Define clear objectives. Start by setting clear goals for the event. What is the purpose of the gathering? Whether it's to educate, celebrate, or inspire, having a clear objective guides every decision—from the guest list to the venue.

Budget wisely. Establish a budget and prioritize spending on essential areas. Always include a contingency fund (typically ten to fifteen percent of the total budget) for unexpected expenses.

Choose the right venue. Location matters! Ensure the venue matches the event's theme and is accessible to your attendees. Consider parking, transportation, and whether the space accommodates all your needs.

Secure vendors early. Whether it's catering, audiovisual equipment, or florists, secure reputable vendors well in advance. Building a list of trusted partners ensures quality and reliability.

Plan for technology. Make sure there's reliable Wi-Fi, adequate lighting, and any necessary tech for presentations. Have a backup plan in case of technical issues.

Create a detailed event schedule. Break down the entire event into smaller, timed segments. Include speakers, meals, and breaks, and be sure to communicate the schedule to all involved.

Prepare for a great guest experience. Ensure all attendees feel welcomed and comfortable. Consider things like good signage, providing programs, and offering refreshments. Small touches can go a long way.

Delegate tasks. Don't try to do everything yourself. Assign responsibilities to team members or trusted volunteers. Having a clear division of labor will prevent last-minute chaos.

Prepare for the unexpected. There's always something that can go wrong, so plan for emergencies. Have a first-aid kit, extra supplies, and contingency plans in place.

Follow up after the event. Thank attendees, vendors, and staff. Request feedback to learn what worked and what can be improved for future events.

Off-Site Meeting Coordination Tips

Plan for pre-meeting communication. Send detailed information about the off-site location, including directions, parking details, and an agenda in advance to all attendees. This reduces confusion on the day of the event.

Ensure accessibility. Confirm that the venue is easily accessible for all participants. This includes considering those with mobility issues, transportation needs, or special requirements.

Set up tech. Ensure the meeting space is equipped with the necessary equipment (projectors, microphones, Wi-Fi, et cetera). Test all tech setups before the meeting starts.

Create a comfortable environment. Make the environment conducive to productivity by providing comfortable seating, good lighting, and quiet spaces for breakout sessions.

Supply refreshments. Provide coffee, water, snacks, or even a meal, depending on the meeting's length. This keeps participants energized and focused throughout the meeting.

Prepare an agenda. A clear agenda is crucial for keeping the meeting on track and ensuring that all necessary points are covered. Share this ahead of time, and stick to it.

Offer breaks. Long meetings can lead to fatigue and disengagement. Schedule breaks for stretching, networking, or a mental reset.

Encourage collaboration. Facilitate opportunities for group discussions and brainstorming. This is particularly important for off-site meetings, where the change of environment should inspire new ideas and collaboration.

Be mindful of time. Respect everyone's time by keeping the meeting on schedule. If a topic needs more discussion, consider following up after the meeting instead of extending the time.

Provide follow-up materials. After the meeting, send out a summary, action items, and any relevant resources. This ensures that the momentum from the meeting continues.

Lessons Learned in Business and Ministry

Building Living The Dream Consultants LLC taught me some powerful lessons:

Obedience trumps opinion. Many people may not understand your vision. You must be obedient to what God has called you to build.

Consistency is key. You cannot build an empire with sporadic efforts. Show up every day—even when no one is clapping.

Systems sustain success. Emotion builds momentum, but systems sustain success. Don't just have dreams—have documentation, timelines, and operational procedures.

Honor the process. Nothing great is built overnight. You must fall in love with the process of growth.

Case Studies: Faith in Action

Here are two real examples of how prioritizing potential produced transformation:

Case Study 1: Ministry to Marketplace

A small church reached out, struggling with disorganization and declining engagement. After a detailed strategic assessment, we:

- Restructured their board.
- Filed for 501(c)(3) compliance.
- Created a full calendar of events.
- Trained their administrative staff.
- Developed community partnerships.

Today, they are thriving with a new sanctuary under construction and an active outreach arm feeding hundreds monthly.

Case Study 2: From Vision to LLC

An aspiring entrepreneur had an idea but no structure. Together, we:

- Filed her business formation documents.
- Built a website and brand identity.
- Created a calendar management system.
- Positioned her for grant funding.

Today, her small business serves clients across three states—and growing.

Both stories prove that strategy and faith working together can produce supernatural results.

Empowering Leaders: My Coaching Philosophy

At Living The Dream Consultants LLC, I don't just offer services—I mentor leaders. I believe in kingdom leadership transformation, where:

- Vision is clarified.
- Values are solidified.
- Structures are sanctified.

My coaching philosophy is simple:

Empower. Equip. Execute. When I coach a client, I empower them with knowledge, equip them with tools, and walk with them until execution happens. Transformation is not an event, it's a process.

I remind leaders that it's not just about what you build—but who you become in the building.

The Role of Faith in Entrepreneurship

Faith is the oxygen of my business.

There were seasons when contracts were slow, when invoices were delayed, and when discouragement knocked loudly. But every time, God provided.

Living The Dream Consultants LLC is an altar. Every client, every project is a form of worship.

I incorporate prayer into my consultations. I pray over my clients' visions. I seek divine strategy, not just human wisdom.

Faith without works is dead, but works without faith are empty. Together, faith and strategy create unstoppable momentum.

A Call to Prioritize Your Potential

You reading this today is not an accident.

You have dreams dormant inside of you. Businesses to launch. Ministries to lead. Books to write. Products to produce.

The question is not whether you have potential, but whether you will prioritize it.

Prioritizing your potential looks like:

- Investing in yourself.
- Building strategic systems.
- Surrounding yourself with accountability.
- Staying anchored in faith.
- Committing to excellence.

It's time to move from idea to implementation, from vision to venture, from potential to purpose.

Conclusion: Living the Dream, Fulfilling the Call

When I started Living The Dream Consultants LLC, I didn't have everything figured out. What I had was a yes in my spirit and a determination to be faithful over little so that God could make me ruler over much.

Every step has required intentionality. Every client has taught me something new. Every contract has been a testimony.

Today, Living The Dream Consultants LLC stands not just as a business but as a beacon for those who dare to believe that their dreams are valid—and with strategy, stewardship, and faith—they are achievable.

Step Boldly Into Your Next Chapter with Living The Dream Consultants LLC

Your vision is too important to leave to chance. At Living The Dream Consultants LLC, we help you build with purpose, plan with precision, and lead with excellence. Together, we will turn your God-given dreams into sustainable realities—because when faith meets strategy, there are no limits to what you can achieve.

Living the Dream is not just a name—it's a destiny. Let's build yours.

Meet the Author | Kathleen Kim Moore

Kathleen Kim Moore is the founder of Living The Dream Consultants LLC, a faith-based consultancy committed to administrative excellence and strategic visioning for businesses and ministries. With more than forty years of leadership experience and a passion for Kingdom order, she equips leaders to build strong foundations, execute with precision, and fulfill their divine potential.

Living the Dream is not just a name—it's a destiny. Let's build yours.

Email: kkimmoore@livingthedream.live

Website: KathleenKimMoore.com

Facebook: Living The Dream Consultants LLC

Instagram: instagram.com/iamkkimmoore

TikTok: tiktok.com/@iamkkimmoore

A Strategic Plan for the Busy Leader

Erika Brooks, LPC, CSAC

Jane has always been a busy woman. She is a business owner who prides herself in helping others with their problems and concerns. She is active in her community and her church. She is involved with many different organizations and projects. She is someone who people often go to when they need help or something to be done. She wears her self-sacrifice as a badge of honor. She loved what she was doing and loved feeling needed, but there were some things that she was missing. She was not having as much time to hang out with her close friends. She had problems sleeping and often felt that she did not get enough rest the night before. She began to miss deadlines or forget to complete tasks. She began to have chronic headaches.

After years of fifty-hour weeks and constant exhaustion, she hit a breaking point. She began talking to a life coach about her feelings of frustration, agitation, and chronic body pains. With coaching, she learned to create a self-care plan to relieve stress and burnout.

In the beginning, it was not always easy to focus on herself, but with time, she got the hang of it. After committing to a regular relaxation plan, including meditation, stretching, and journaling, she found she could lead with greater clarity, compassion, and creativity. She began to function more effectively and found her smile again.

This is not a fictional person; Jane is me. As the saying goes, I was burning the candle at both ends—and up the middle. I found myself frustrated that others weren't working as hard as me. What got me to the point of making a change was seeing that I was helping others take care of themselves, but I was still missing happiness and joy. I started to wonder if work was all there was to life. As I was journaling about finding happiness, I realized, I deserved to be as happy as my clients and others around me. Investing in my well-being is not a detour from success; it is the fast track to it.

You can be wildly ambitious, incredibly disciplined, and fiercely committed to your goals, but if you neglect self-care, your success will eventually come at a cost. Too many high achievers are celebrated for pushing themselves beyond their limits, but behind the scenes, they are exhausted, unfulfilled, and often burnt out. In truth, self-care is not a luxury. It is not selfish. It is not an afterthought. Self-care is a strategic, foundational part of sustainable success.

Consider this: According to a 2023 report by the World Health Organization, burnout is now classified as an occupational phenomenon, affecting more than sixty percent of working professionals globally. These numbers are not simply about feeling "tired"; they reflect a profound disconnection from joy, creativity, and fulfillment—the very engines that drive success.

This chapter is an invitation to shift your mindset: self-care is not what you do when everything is done; it is what enables you to get things done and to do them well. Here, we will explore why self-care matters, how to build it into your daily routine, and how it fuels the strength, focus, and resilience you need to reach your full potential.

Rethinking Self-Care

The world often sells self-care as bubble baths, candles, and spa days. While these things are nice and can be part of a wellness routine, real self-care goes deeper than that. It is about consistently meeting your mental, physical, emotional, and spiritual needs so you can function at your best.

True self-care is often unglamorous. It looks like getting enough sleep, saying no to overcommitments, going to therapy, setting boundaries with toxic people, or stepping away from your phone to be present with your family. It is about maintaining your capacity to show up for your life and your goals with clear vision and strength.

High performers in various areas, including athletes, executives, entrepreneurs, and artists prioritize self-care because they understand a fundamental truth: Your body, mind, and spirit are at the core of your productivity. If you don't maintain the engine, you won't make it to the destination.

Self-care is also a key component of self-respect. It is a way of saying, "I matter. My well-being is not negotiable." When you consistently honor your needs, you affirm your own worth and that you operate from a place of strength, not weakness.

The Cost of Neglecting Self-Care

Neglecting self-care doesn't just affect your mood or energy—it compromises your ability to succeed. When you constantly pour out without replenishing yourself, the consequences show up in every area of life: poor decision-making, emotional reactivity, chronic stress, strained relationships, and health issues.

In the short term, you may feel like you're gaining ground by skipping meals, pushing through exhaustion, or saying yes to every request.

But long-term, this approach leads to burnout, disconnection, and decreased performance.

You can't pour from an empty cup. And if you keep pushing without pausing, your body or your mind will eventually force you to stop. The question is not whether you need self-care; it's whether you will choose it intentionally or wait until you have no other choice.

Building Your Self-Care Strategy

As I said earlier, my self-care journey was not easy in the beginning. For some reason, I was still trying to hold on to my Superwoman cape and save the world, but the constant headaches said that someone else would have to fulfill the role of Superwoman.

I began my plan by spending time thinking of what is important to me. If you know me, you know that my family and *framily*—friends who are like family—are the most important to me. To make sure I fulfilled that, I made sure to carve time out for them whether it be to make sure I talk to them on the phone or see them in person. Sundays are the days for church and the day that I make sure to spend face-to-face time with my parents. I try to make sure to call my friends during the week after work. I also make sure to schedule a day a month in which I can do absolutely nothing. I make sure to mark this day on my calendar just as I do any other appointment.

Speaking of appointments, I make sure to schedule my annual health appointments—and any others as needed. One part of self-care is taking care of your health. This can include taking medications, getting health exams, and even going to therapy. As part of my plan, I spoke with my neurologist about my migraines and what the best treatment plan was for me. Because I was skipping meals to get work done, I spoke with a dietitian/nutritionist who helped me create meal ideas so that I was making sure to get proper nutrition. I also made sure to get proper hydration—at least sixty-four ounces of water.

My providers also encouraged me to get physical. I have never been big on exercising, but I found activities that I enjoy such as walking, dancing, and yoga. My goal is thirty minutes of exercise five days a week. Some days, I listen to a playlist while I walk; other days I listen to a podcast that is of interest to me. I learned that walks clear my mind and the yoga helps to release tension in my body.

The biggest change came in the area of sleep. I began to practice good sleep hygiene, meaning I make sure conditions are optimal for good sleep—setting a reasonable, regular bedtime and wake-up time, setting the room to a comfortable temperature, not working in bed, decreasing fluid intake at a reasonable time, and decreasing the blue light in my room. I also began using aromatherapy in my bedroom to make it more inviting for sleep—lavender and chamomile are amazing for sleep!

Other parts of my plan: I journal, read daily affirmations, and continue to pray. I take breaks at work, and when I feel I need it, I take advantage of my leave time. I also decided that I deserved some of the stereotypical self-care ideas, such as getting my mani/pedis and facials on a regular basis. I also made small changes such as using my Do Not Disturb on my phone and allowing calls to go to voicemail. I don't push myself to respond to messages until I am ready to versus when others feel I should. I also gave myself permission to accept help when needed.

In the beginning, it was hard to follow this plan because I had gotten into a habit of not taking care of myself and was running on autopilot. Now, my plan is second nature to me. I don't have to think about it. There were some things I noticed quickly, including feeling like I had more energy, less tension, and I was able to think clearer. I was also able to rebound quicker from challenges at work. Also, I began to be more effective with my time and able to be more creative with my work/services.

Now, keep in mind, this plan is what worked for me. Your plan may—and probably will—look different. It should be specific to your wants, needs, and likes. To create a successful self-care plan, it must become intentional and consistent. Here's how to build a plan that works:

1. **Know your core needs.** Start by identifying your most essential needs in these four areas:
   - **Physical:** sleep, nutrition, hydration, exercise, rest
     - *How much sleep and rest do you need to feel refueled? What type of exercise do you enjoy? What type of diet is best for you?*
   - **Emotional:** connection, expression, support
     - *What relationships fill you? What relationships drain you? How are you expressing your feelings? How do you pay attention to your thoughts and emotions? Who is included in your support system?*
   - **Mental:** focus, stimulation, downtime
     - *What are you focused on? How do you spend your downtime? How much downtime do you allow yourself?*
   - **Spiritual:** peace, meaning, faith practices
     - *How do you honor your spirituality? What is you spiritual practice? What does your spirituality mean to you?*

Take inventory: Which areas are you nurturing, and which are being neglected? Awareness is the first step to change.

Self-Care Self-Assessment

On a scale of 1 to 5 (1=rarely, 5=consistently), rate yourself:

- I get seven to eight hours of sleep per night.

- I eat balanced, nutritious meals daily.
- I move my body regularly (at least three times per week).
- I engage in activities that bring me joy.
- I have supportive relationships I can lean on.
- I set healthy boundaries with work, technology, and people.
- I have daily quiet time for reflection, prayer, or meditation.
- I actively manage stress (e.g., breathing exercises, mindfulness).
- I seek help or support when needed (therapy, mentorship).
- I take regular breaks and vacations without guilt.

Scoring

- 40–50: You have a strong self-care foundation. Keep nurturing it!
- 25–39: You are mindful of self-care but have some areas for growth.
- 10–24: Your self-care needs attention. Prioritize small, sustainable changes now.

2. **Choose daily nonnegotiables.** Pick two to three simple, powerful practices that you commit to daily. For example:
   - Drink sixty-four ounces of water.
   - Move your body for twenty minutes.
   - Journal or pray every morning.
   - Turn off your phone an hour before bed.

These non-negotiables act like anchors, grounding you, no matter how busy life gets.

3. **Integrate, don't add on.** Self-care should feel like support, not another task. Look for ways to weave it into what you already do:
   ○ Stretch while watching TV.
   ○ Take walking meetings.
   ○ Practice gratitude while brushing your teeth.

Remember: Small, consistent actions create lasting change.

4. **Protect your energy.** Boundaries are essential to sustainable success. Say no when needed. Create tech-free zones. Prioritize rest without guilt. Recognize that energy management is as important as time management. Energy is finite. Where you spend it determines what you build. Be selective. Be wise.

As I have been working my self-care plan, people noticed I was saying no more often. In the beginning, this was difficult as I was a people pleaser, but in pleasing others, I was sometimes dishonoring me. Saying no to requests gave me more free time and time to relax. This also gave others the opportunity to display their talents.

The Ripple Effects of Self-Care

When you prioritize self-care, the benefits ripple out into every part of your life:

- You think more clearly and make better decisions.'
- You respond to stress with more calm and confidence.
- You have more stamina to pursue long-term goals.
- You cultivate deeper relationships with others.

Self-care doesn't just benefit you; it benefits everyone around you. When you are energized, joyful, and healthy, you are more available to support, inspire, and serve others. Your creativity flourishes. Your leadership skills strengthen. Your presence becomes a gift.

Conclusion

My journey with self-care is far from over; actually, this is just the beginning. I realize that this is not a race and that as I continue to grow, my plan may be revisited and will be adjusted as needed. Taking the time to care for self has improved my health, mental clarity, and focus. I feel happier and more relaxed. My confidence has begun to soar as well. Lastly, my business/work has not suffered from me taking care of myself, rather it has grown.

Success that comes at the expense of your health, joy, or peace is not true success. When you make self-care a nonnegotiable part of your life, you give yourself the energy, clarity, and resilience to sustain your success over the long haul.

You are your most valuable asset. Prioritize your well-being like your future depends on it because it does. Remember, your potential is not just about what you can achieve. It's about who you become when you are fully supported, fully present, and fully alive.

Here are some questions I encourage you to reflect on and spend some time exploring:

- What are three self-care practices I can commit to daily?
- Where in my life do I need stronger boundaries to protect my energy?
- What limiting beliefs do I need to release about rest, worthiness, or productivity?

Self-care is not a reward for success. It is the strategy that makes true, lasting success possible.

I leave you with this challenge: Today, choose one small act of self-care and treat it like the essential priority it is. Your future self is depending on you.

Wishing you an exciting self-care journey.

Meet the Author | Erika Brooks

Erika Brooks is a licensed professional counselor and certified substance abuse counselor in Richmond, Virginia. She is the owner of Enlightenment Counseling Services, LLC, helping people with mental health concerns, including mood disorders, grief, trauma, self-care, and women's issues. She has been a guest speaker on various podcasts and conferences. She is the coauthor of four anthologies and a writer for *HOPE* magazine.

The Seasoning of My Foundation
Wanda L. Washington

Before anything can grow, it needs something to grow from. My foundation was shaped by the three people who left the deepest imprint on my life: my grandmother, mother, and father. Together, they formed a triangle, each offering something different. Over time, those lessons became the base I would build on. Surrounding that base were my brothers and sisters, a close-knit circle of influence whose consistent support and steady presence were always there.

That truth was first planted in me by my paternal grandmother, a woman anchored in solid family values, quiet strength, and unwavering faith. Her life wasn't built on only titles—*Mama*—but on integrity, discipline, and grace. She didn't teach by lecture. She taught by example through her hands, eyes, presence, and how she cared for everyone around her.

One Thanksgiving, I asked her how she made her famous dressing. It was always the first thing gone from the table. She shared the ingredients, and when I asked how much of each, she just said, "Add a little bit of this, and a pinch of that, and taste it." That was it. At first, I wasn't sure if it would work, but I followed her instructions, and to my surprise, it came out well. That was her teaching me to trust the recipe and my intuition. Whether in the kitchen or life, she taught me to work with what I had, trust my instincts, and season things with care and grace.

My mother carries a pure heart, quiet strength, and unconditional love. She embodies grace without saying a word, in the way she moves—gentle, steady, and never in a rush. She doesn't need to speak loudly for you to feel her presence. Her love is in the smallest things: warming a plate of food before you even ask and knowing when you need comfort without a word spoken. She's the kind of woman who leads by example and not by instructions. She will give her last to someone else and smile as though she were giving them a gift from her heart. Her grace isn't about performance; it is who she is. She is soft-spoken, but her presence lingers. You feel her long after she's left the room. It's not what she says, it's how she makes you feel. The kind of strength that wraps around you like a warm blanket when you don't even realize you are cold.

For a long time, I thought my quiet nature was shyness. But over the years, I've realized what I saw as quiet was my mother's soul living in me. I don't just resemble her in how I look. I mimic her spirit. The steady, thoughtful way I move through the world? That's my mother's legacy at work.

From her, I've learned that real love is quiet, and strength is steady. Showing up with grace is one of the most powerful things a woman can do.

And then there are my brothers.

My mother always said, "Watch out for your sisters," and they did. But not always in a way I expected or wanted. I still remember how frustrated I was when they insisted I change the tire and oil in my car. I realize it was the way Mom instilled love in them to love, protect, and prepare me, but in their loving way. Through them, I know how to move safely in the world. They were building a kind of support system I now rely on.

A father's presence in a girl's life is immeasurable. My father shaped how I see the world in a way no one else could. He was grounded, instinctive, deeply in tune with the land, the sky, and the trees. Nature taught him how to live, and he passed that lens on to me. He gave direction, not just through rules, but through revelation. He helped me see how everything in life is connected.

He revealed nature in a way that made it more than scenery; it became a teacher. He used to say, "Watch how animals behave. You'll learn everything about people, timing, and survival." He showed me how to look deeper, to ask what the wind, the stillness, or the movement of animals might be trying to tell me. Through him, I learned to pay attention to the patterns others missed; to think critically, observe with intention, and discern what lies beneath the surface.

He didn't just show me nature, he taught me how to read life. He was real, outspoken, and rooted in truth. His lessons weren't always spoken; they were in how he moved through the world, and expected me to move the same way.

When I got my first apartment, he looked me in the eye and said, "This is your peace. Protect it." That stuck with me. It wasn't just about a space, it was about guarding my spirit, mind, and sense of self.

But the strongest gift he gave me was my voice. I found it through him. He taught me how to be a lady, but also how to speak with conviction, to lead without apology, and to remain calm in the middle of chaos. He once told me, "You are a leader." And in that moment, something clicked. I believed it because he did. He didn't just speak to who I was, but who I could become.

My sisters have rich, soulful, unforgettable voices that can silence a room. Music flowed through them like second nature. While I didn't sing like they did, I saw something else: a way to bring their gifts into the world with a close family friend. I formed a group and began managing them. I scheduled rehearsals, booked local gigs, handled the communication, and coordinated our image and direction. I was still young, but I was learning fast, learning to prioritize not just talent, but time, planning, and execution.

That experience taught me to manage people, see ahead, and organize behind the scenes without losing sight of the vision. I was beginning to understand what it meant to activate potential, not just in others, but in myself.

That same clarity showed up when I took on directing a state pageant. I had no formal training, but I had determination and a deep belief in possibility. I fundraised, promoted, recruited contestants, secured a venue, coordinated entertainment, sold advertisements, and designed the guidebook while managing expectations and logistics. What I'm most proud of is the opening composition. I hired an African dance company and asked for a custom drumbeat as each contestant entered. The energy was electric. The crowd was moved. It was bold, cultural, beautiful—and it worked.

I was applying leadership and how to bring a vision to life while delivering results, not just ideas.

After two decades of running my business, those lessons remain with me—still building, growing, and seasoning what was passed down to me. The foundation laid by my family—their values, lessons, and the strength they imparted—is not a static inheritance. It's something I continue to shape and refine. And I know now: the legacy isn't just what I've inherited; it's what I choose to leave behind and share with others. It's a living, breathing gift that grows with me, expands with every lesson, and evolves with every step.

The Seasoning of My Foundation

The ingredients of my family's love, wisdom, and guidance have seasoned me, I now pass those ingredients on. They are vision, hope, joy, life experiences, action, and an openness to embrace growth in your own sweet time.

This brings us to a critical point: It's more than setting goals, it's about recognizing what already lives inside of you, honoring the people who shaped you, and boldly stepping into your capacity to grow. Within you lies a treasure chest of possibilities just waiting to be unlocked. This journey of growth is intentional.

Start with a vision. A vision is the compass that directs every step you take. It's the mental picture of the person you want to become, the life you want to lead. Without a clear vision, it's easy to drift or get distracted by the noise around you. A vision is more than just a goal, it's an alignment of your heart, mind, and actions toward a purpose that excites and fulfills you. It's the destination, the "why" behind everything you do.

In my journey, I've had moments where the path wasn't clear. I've had to develop a vision for what I wanted to do and who I wanted to be. My father's lessons about nature and observation have helped me build a lens through which I can see the possibilities in the world around me. I've begun to ask myself, *What excites me? What am I truly passionate about? What do I want my life to stand for?*

For me, it isn't just about external success. It's about having peace in my choices and alignment in my actions. My life vision is rooted in a fundamental belief: I am building something meaningful.

Hope is what keeps us going when the road gets tough. It's the belief that what lies ahead is worth the effort, even when things don't unfold as expected. Hope is not passive; it's active, requiring you to take deliberate steps forward, even when the path seems uncertain.

In my journey, I'm building a life that reflects my values, dreams, and passions. Whether it was starting my business or leading a pageant, there were moments when it seemed impossible. But the hope that I could make a difference kept me moving forward.

For anyone looking to prioritize their potential, hope is essential. It breathes life into our dreams and courage into our setbacks. It gives us something to hold on to when things feel uncertain. Hope keeps the vision alive, even when progress is slow, and when we face the hard moments, it reminds us that we still have the strength to keep going.

While vision and hope fuel your path, joy is the energy that sustains you throughout the journey. It's the inner sense of fulfillment you get when you align with what truly excites you and create something that resonates with your heart. Without joy, prioritizing your potential can feel like a chore instead of a calling.

Joy doesn't always come in big moments; it's often found in the small wins, moments when you take a step closer to your goal and feel truly alive in what you're doing. Joy has been seeing my business grow, knowing it's something I created from nothing. I was deeply moved, watching my sisters use their voices to inspire others. It's been in moments of quiet reflection that I'm on the right path, even when things are difficult.

As I reflect on the seasons of my life, I realize that my growth has been shaped by my experiences. The trials, triumphs, failures, and lessons have all added depth to my understanding of what it takes to reach my full potential.

For me, prioritizing my potential has meant learning to trust my instincts, just as my grandmother taught me with her recipes. She showed me that life doesn't always have clear instructions, and you must trust yourself to add a little bit of this and a pinch of that. Life requires flexibility, adaptability, and faith in your own intuition.

It's also meant that growth is not always linear. The path to realizing your potential will often take unexpected paths. Embrace those twists and turns. They're seasoning your journey, making you more capable, resilient, and prepared for the next step.

Vision, hope, and joy are the foundation. But none of them are enough if they aren't followed by action. Prioritizing your potential means making choices that align with your goals, vision, and values. It's not enough to *wish* for success. You have to *work* for it.

As I worked on building my past business adventures, managing my sisters, and directing the pageant, I learned that there's no substitute for hard work. Yes, vision is critical. Hope will get you through the tough times. And joy will keep you energized. But the one thing that holds it all together is consistent action. When you take action—no matter how small—you are telling the world and yourself that you are committed to your potential.

Finally, prioritizing your potential is about embracing the journey of becoming. We are all works in progress. To unlock your fullest potential, you must be willing to evolve, to adapt, and to learn from each experience. This is where your seasoning truly comes into play. Each experience, whether it's a victory or a lesson learned from failure, adds to your wisdom and prepares you for the next chapter.

As I reflect on the woman I am today, I realize that I am the sum of all the lessons learned, all the seasons lived, and every bit of seasoning I've added along the way. I've learned how to trust my instincts, to take action even in uncertainty, and to grow into the leader I never imagined I could become. Through it all, I've built a business that serves, teaches, and heals. I've walked alongside women on their hair journeys, mentored new professionals, and poured what I've learned into the hands of aspiring businesswomen, planting seeds in others just as others once did for me.

I was eighteen when my father looked me in the eye and said, "You are a leader." I believed him, not because I had proven anything yet, but because I trusted his eyes. I trusted the way he saw me—that was his vision of my potential. In that moment, a seed was planted. I didn't have a full understanding of what leadership required, but something in me accepted it. That's how potential works: Someone speaks it over you, and even if you don't fully grasp it, the words take root. Over the years, that seed was watered by challenges, experiences, and moments that demanded I show up and lead. I didn't grow into it overnight. I grew into it through showing up, making mistakes, making decisions, and learning to trust my voice. Now, looking back, I realize I didn't just believe my father, I became the woman he already saw.

And now, as I step into a new chapter, I carry that growth with intention. I'm devoting this next season to helping others recognize the potential within themselves, to speak life into future leaders the way my father spoke into me—through coaching, mentorship, and lived wisdom. I want to create the kind of space where potential doesn't just get recognized, it gets realized. This is the work I choose to shape.

With Love,
Wanda L. Washington
Keep building.
Keep becoming.
Your legacy is already unfolding.

Meet the Author | Wanda L. Washington

Wanda L. Washington is a master cosmetologist, scalp and haircare educator, and owner-operator of Natural Beauty Boutique LLC, an educational salon devoted to the proper care and empowerment of natural hair. With a career spanning more than two decades, Wanda has helped transform the way women care for and understand their textured hair through education, mentorship, and holistic salon experiences.

A certified Sisterlocks™ consultant and former Sisterlocks™ senior trainer, Wanda has led professional trainings nationwide in advanced loc techniques. She is also a former state trainer for AT&T, where she served as a customer service manager, blending corporate leadership with her passion for development and education.

Wanda is the creator and host of *How Deep is Your Beauty?*, an educational show that explores beauty from the inside out, connecting self-care, scalp health, and personal growth.

Through hands-on instruction, digital education, or direct client care, Wanda continues to pour into the next generation of professionals while helping others embrace their natural beauty, rooted in intention, education, and legacy.

Website: naturalbeautyboutique.com
Email: info@naturalbeautyboutique.com
Instagram: instagram.com/wanda2403/
Facebook: facebook.com/wanda.washington.71/

Prioritizing Your Potential in the Storm

Dr. Nina R. Copeland

Leadership is tested in disruption. Prioritizing your potential during uncertain times is what distinguishes a leader from a titleholder. Earning titles like executive, owner, manager, or a high-ranking military officer certifies that you have mastered your craft. Moreover, you receive a substantial salary.

Life is good. Yet, just as you reach the pinnacle of your career, the unexpected occurs—a shift. It often feels like a storm that shakes your confidence, challenges your direction, and forces you to confront questions you never expected to ask yourself. It disrupts the version of leadership you mastered and makes you wonder if your pursuit of success has quietly sacrificed your growth. Now, you find yourself struggling to stay steady. Your ability to make sound decisions is becoming more uncertain. You are caught in a tug-of-war between destiny and what you see as defeat. Your purpose, not just your position, has changed, and you are being pulled by a greater cause into the unknown, all while fighting fiercely to return to what you once believed defined and validated you as a leader. You are now in unexplored territory.

Why now? Where do I go from here? Should I give up? These questions race through your mind—questions you never thought would come up. I understand this deeply. I have lived it.

I was thriving in my career. My path was clear, my reputation was solid, and my influence was well-established. I climbed the ranks with grace, consistency, and determination. Promotions came regularly. My decisions were trusted. I was producing results. I was proud of the work and confident in my leadership. Everything around me confirmed that I was aligned with my purpose—until one day, it was not.

What began as subtle discomfort evolved into a restructuring that left me without the title I had faithfully served. The shift felt personal. Suddenly, I was no longer leading the meetings or making decisions. I was outside of the system I had mastered. I could not tell anyone who I was when the door to the military was abruptly closing.

Disruption for high-achieving leaders is often a silent, disorienting, and internal storm that no one prepares you for. Your position will not shield you from disruption. In fact, the higher you climb, the more subjective you become. You take classes, read books, attend seminars, et cetera, on how to manage a crisis, lead with confidence, and become agile and adaptable, all of which help you mask externally what is tearing you apart internally. At first glance, my life still appeared steadily, but internally, I was unraveling, falling into a depression. When life hits that hard, you can't go back to who you were before. That's when I met the pivot. Not the pivot I planned. The pivot I resisted. The pivot I needed to take me to the next level.

The truth is, every leader will experience this moment—the one where your titles will no longer sustain you, your metrics no longer motivate you, and your success feels more like a burden than a blessing. This is the threshold of reinvention. This is where you stop asking, *How can I maintain?* and start asking, *What am I becoming?* The becoming is your real purpose. It is calling you to your next level, not to do more, but to live more fully. That part can be disorienting. Most leaders find themselves standing in a space that feels dim, unfamiliar, and unsteady. It is often quiet there, no applause, no confirmation, and no certainty—just you, your questions, and the subtle pull of something more.

In that space, it's tempting to retreat. To return to what's proven. To rebuild what feels safe. You want to reach for the version of yourself that once worked, knew the rules, delivered the results, and earned respect. But growth doesn't wait for comfort. And your future won't fit inside your former framework.

This is where you learn to prioritize your potential over your past performance. To move beyond the image, you must reconnect with the truth you carry. The shift isn't about striving. It's about shedding, not about improving what was, but discovering authentic power.

That is where evolution begins. Quietly. Internally. Authentically. And once it starts, you realize you are not losing yourself. You are finally meeting who you were always meant to be in your new chapter of life.

For corporate leaders, stepping away from a role is more than just a career change. It's an identity crisis that's rarely discussed. The hard truth is the responsibilities, recognition, and influence become so intertwined with who you are that when they're gone, you barely recognize yourself.

You start to wonder if your value has expired. Those thoughts creep in and take root, growing into something heavy and hard to shake. You question whether your skills still matter. You begin to ask yourself, *Who am I without the access, the leadership position, and the expectations?* This is where impostor syndrome shows up. Loud.

It's wild how quickly you forget. You forget the breakthroughs. The late nights. The growth. You forget the voice that led rooms and shaped outcomes. All of that begins to fade when your identity has been wrapped around a role for so long. Let me tell you a secret: You can use those same skills to build something far greater. It may take extra effort. However, you can start again. This is when you must decide if you will anchor your identity in your title, or you will rise above the storm by choosing to prioritize your potential.

When you have poured everything into a professional journey, you stop checking in with your purpose, passion, and needs. In the military, it was mission first, no matter what. Period.

I had to sit still and ask, *What do I truly want next?* That's where the heavy lifting began. The inner work is different. It takes a high level of emotional intelligence to play inside with your thoughts, feelings, and emotions. It's a personal operation called soul work—when you go deep and examine the root cause of your thoughts, challenge the narratives you have carried, and release some of the cognitive distortions. Take time to rewrite your story.

I learned that your identity and worth have never been rooted in a title. They live in your character, your quiet resilience, and the truth of who you are when no one is watching. It's that version of you—the grounded, authentic you—that must lead the way forward. That realization changed everything. I was not failing. I was being redirected. Leadership is not just about weathering storms; it is about recognizing when the boat is no longer designed to take you where you need to go.

When navigating a transition, you are not starting from scratch; you are building on experience. The hardest leap for someone to take is to leave a corporation for entrepreneurship. The mental shift is fundamental. What I learned is that it's not an overnight process, and it takes time. It took me approximately two years to fully walk in my authenticity. The moment you stop trying to return to what was and begin to ask what is possible, you reclaim your power. Your skills, decisions, and leadership moments were not wasted. They were preparing you for something more aligned. I did not lose my voice; I needed a new platform to use it.

Here are five great things to consider as you navigate your transition and prioritize your potential for a new version of yourself.

1. Grief in Disguise

Even when it's planned, even when it's on your terms, stepping away from a leadership role can feel like a loss. It's not just the work, it's identity, the rhythm, the sense of purpose that's been part of your life for years. The ache you feel. It's grief, and it's real.

How to Overcome: Let yourself grieve. Don't bury it under busy work or bravado. Say it out loud. Write about it. Talk to someone who understands what this transition feels like. This isn't weakness. It's the cost of having cared deeply. And honoring that helps you move forward whole.

2. Isolation

The quiet after leadership can be jarring. Calls slow down. Your name isn't in the room as often. People aren't quite sure how to engage now that you're not "the boss." That shift in social dynamics can feel like a slow fade into invisibility.

How to Overcome: Reach out. Don't wait for others to bridge the gap—lead again, this time by choosing connection over silence. Build a new circle that sees *you*, not your title. Join groups, mentor others, and reconnect with relationships that were always about more than power.

3. Uncertainty

You have been the one with answers. Now you're staring into a foggy future, wondering what's next. That pressure to "figure it out" can sit heavy, especially when the old markers of success no longer apply.

How to Overcome: Give yourself permission to explore. This isn't a problem to solve. It's a season to live through. Get curious about what energizes you now. Play. Reflect. Try without having to commit. Uncertainty isn't your enemy—it's your invitation to reimagine.

4. Questioning

You start to wonder: *Was it really me making the difference, or was I riding the wave of a strong system?* Without the usual wins and applause, self-doubt creeps in. That once-solid confidence starts to crack.

How to Overcome: Pause and remember what you brought to the table—your vision, your resilience, your capacity to lead through the unknown. That didn't disappear with the role. Reconnect with your receipts, the moments no one could have pulled off but you.

5. Opportunity

Yes, the opportunity is out there, but let's be honest: You cannot fully step into what's next if you're still trying to recreate what was. Transformation demands release. You've got to let go of what's no longer aligned.

How to Overcome: Make space—internally and externally. Clear the clutter of old expectations. Let go of trying to replicate your past. Be open to the unexpected. Say yes to stretch experiences. This next season won't look like the last, and that's not just okay; it might be precisely what you need.

Becoming the Leader You Were Meant to Be

The next level of leadership requires less proving and more positioning. It demands less performance and more presence. This is the work that transforms disruption into development.

When I stopped clinging to outdated expectations and started honoring my unique strengths, everything shifted. I no longer led for affirmation. I led from alignment. Leadership after disruption requires a willingness to pause, the discipline to reflect, and the courage to realign. I noticed the quiet brilliance in what I had always done well: coaching, casting vision, connecting leaders, and cultivating growth. Determine your quiet brilliance and take a B.O.L.D. stance.

B.O.L.D. is my signature framework to help people move into the next season. Additionally, it serves as a reminder that your potential does not require permission; only your participation is needed.

Believe in yourself and refuse to doubt. When the title is gone and no one is watching, you still must believe in yourself. Not because it all makes sense, but because you are still valuable. Your worth is not connected to a position or a platform. It is rooted in your identity. Your potential lives in who you are, not in what you do.

Optimize your current situation and seek advancement. That means making the most of where you are right now. You may not have everything you want, but you have something you can use. There is always a next step, always a lesson hidden in the middle of the struggle. Growth does not wait until you feel ready; it responds when you move, so do not stay stuck. Ask yourself: *What is this moment trying to show me? What can I shift, strengthen, or stretch so I can move forward from here?'*

Liberate yourself from self-limiting beliefs. Shed the narratives that no longer serve you. Release the weight of impostor syndrome, perfectionism, and old definitions of success that keep you stuck.

Dare to be different. Leadership isn't about fitting in. It's about standing in your uniqueness and being bold enough to lead in a way that is true to who you are, not who others expect you to be.

For high-level leaders and entrepreneurs, B.O.L.D. action is not about chasing impulsive moves or reckless risks. It's about making intentional, purpose-driven decisions that move your leadership, business, and life forward with clarity. Bold action is the courage to say yes to a new direction, even when the path is unfamiliar and the outcome is not guaranteed. It is the wisdom to release what no longer aligns, even if it is what once made you successful. It is the discipline to launch what you have been sitting on, not because every detail is perfect, but because growth demands movement, not permission. B.O.L.D. action is also about elevating your standards, protecting your energy, and communicating your boundaries. It's about showing up with a stronger voice, a more refined vision, and a deeper conviction. Bold leadership is decisive leadership. It requires you to stop negotiating out of fear and start aligning with your purpose. The next level is not waiting for perfection. It is waiting for a decision. This is how you move through the storm. This is how you prioritize your potential.

As a leadership coach, my focus is on helping high-performing professionals who are no longer fulfilled by titles or roles that once defined them. They find themselves in unfamiliar territory, still capable, still brilliant, but searching for clarity and alignment. I walk with them through that space and help them shift from striving to becoming. My coaching helps leaders pause, reflect, and reimagine what is possible when they stop chasing validation and start prioritizing their potential.

I use the DISC behavioral assessment to help my clients understand how they lead, how they communicate, and how they respond to pressure. This tool brings clarity to how they show up in the world and gives them language to lead more effectively. I also take a strengths-based approach that helps them uncover what is already working within them so they can lead from a place of truth rather than performance. My work is not just strategy. It is personal. It is purpose-driven.

I help leaders release outdated expectations and reconnect with the version of themselves that has been buried under the weight of responsibility and routine. They learn how to create from who they are, not just from what they have done. This is where alignment begins. This is where clarity returns. This is where true leadership is born. My mission is to help every leader I work with rise not by doing more, but by becoming more of who they were always meant to be. When they choose to prioritize their potential, everything begins to shift.

Meet the Author | Dr. Nina R. Copeland

Dr. Nina Copeland is a proven leader, strategist, and connector with more than twenty-one years of distinguished service as a military officer. She specializes in leadership development, personal growth, and resilience, equipping executives and teams with the skills to excel under pressure. She holds a master's degree in procurement and acquisition management from Webster University and certifications from the T.I.U.A. School of Business and the John C. Maxwell Leadership Program. Dr. Copeland trained and led more than 10,000 Department of Defense personnel during her military career, strengthening their leadership capabilities and mission readiness. As a Master Resiliency and DISC–certified trainer, she continues empowering professionals by enhancing their ability to lead confidently, improving communication, and building high-performing teams.

Dr. Copeland, an acclaimed author of three bestsellers and an international speaker, challenges professionals to redefine success, embrace resilience, and drive meaningful results. As the founder of Copeland's Coaching and Consulting, she partners with executives and organizations to optimize leadership performance, improve workplace culture, and create lasting impact.

The Confidence Activator

Sharvette Mitchell

W*ow. It was easy to get here,* I thought as I pulled into the parking lot of the Delta Hotel in Colonial Heights, Virginia. It was about 12:45 p.m. on that Saturday, and I was popping in to see one of my Platform Builder clients who was hosting her first one-day conference.

She didn't know that I was coming, and I wanted to keep it that way. I told my friend who also was the event manager, "*Shhh.* Don't tell her I am coming."

She said, "What time will you get there?"

I responded that I would come during lunch so that I could slide in at a time that would not disrupt the conference.

As I got out of my SUV, I pulled out my phone and started recording a quick video so that I could create a reel for Facebook, Instagram, and TikTok. I wanted to make sure I captured this moment—as I heard Certified Master Neuroscience Coach Rachel Luna say, "Your life is *content.*"

Here's what the parking lot video said: "Hey, y'all. So I am heading into the Delta Hotel by Marriott because one of our amazing Platform Builder clients, Dana Wilson, is hosting her first conference. She is the CEO of Hair Cares Inc., and she's a trichologist and SisterLocks educator. And she doesn't know I'm coming! This is totally just for moral support, and so I'm gonna surprise her and stop in. All right, I'm bringing y'all along. Okay. Bye."

As I walked into this newly renovated hotel with its blue graphic carpet and beautiful light fixtures, I was immediately proud of my client. I was met at the door with her custom retractable banner in her brand colors of wine and sage/lime green. The welcome and registration table was also branded with a custom tablecloth and overlay. I saw some of my other Platform Builder clients who were there to volunteer and support the conference host.

As a side note: It always makes me smile when I see my clients partnering and forming bonds together independent of anything I have curated through a program. Here's what I know for sure: Guided support and a safe community are ingredients to growth.

After I greeted a few people, I was on a mission to find my client. I pulled out my phone and recorded another short video, which said, "We're here, we're here. All right. Okay, so I'm inside the hotel. Now I gotta go find Dana. Let's see...they're at lunch. Oh, I see her."

As I entered the actual conference room, the atmosphere was full of good vibes. DJ Shanghi, a local girl DJ, was spinning those line dances and keeping the energy flowing. Several conference guests were on the "dance floor" doing the "Boots on the Ground" line dance. For the record, I cannot get the steps to that line dance to save my life!

That's when I saw Dana across the room and walked up and said, "Surprise."

Yes, she was surprised!

As the conference continued with a panel discussion and then Dana's afternoon presentation, I sat there super proud of her. Every detail was thought of and executed wonderfully. I remember coaching her on this conference when it was just a thought. I have personally hosted nine conferences, and I know the blood, sweat, and maybe tears that go into delivering a quality event. Here she was with a full room and attendees who had traveled from various places to attend her first conference.

I heard Ashley Kirkwood of Speak Your Way to Cash® say that some people get a mentor, but they themselves never become the mentee. Dana is an example of a client (among several others) who has truly become my mentee. If Coach Sharvette gives her a play, she runs the play. She is an action taker, and the earth responds to action takers.

Later on during the conference, she offered a program to her conference attendees, and they could not pull their credit cards out fast enough to enroll in her six-month program. This solidified that her expertise, personal branding, marketing skills, program development, and launch strategy all worked.

Here is the realization that I have...

I am a leader who is assigned to and works best with other leaders. I am a mentor and not just a marketer.

I activate the potential in others through my business coaching focused on clarity and confidence-building. Often, I see the potential in others, and I just need to help them see it in themselves. Once they see the potential, they need to activate it and prioritize it.

Seeing Potential

Many people are walking around with unseen brilliance, not because it's not there, but because no one ever validated it.

That statement may feel like an "Ouch!" or an "Amen!"

For years, you may have been waiting on someone to say, "You've got something special." You may have been hoping a spouse, partner, boss, mentor, family member, or even a friend would look at you and confirm what deep down you already knew—that you were meant for more. That there's greatness in you. That you don't just have potential but you have *purpose.*

But here's the truth: Brilliance doesn't disappear just because it's been ignored. It may be buried, dimmed, or covered by self-doubt, but it's still there waiting to be acknowledged by the most important person in the room: *you.*

Validation is powerful. Let's admit it: Some of us crave it, not because we're weak, but because we're wired for connection. We want to know our gifts matter. We want someone to *see* us. But the danger comes when we attach our value to external affirmation. When we let unspoken validation become the silent thief of our future.

Guess what? There are people who can run a business with their eyes closed, create magic from scratch, speak life into others, and still say, "I don't know if I'm ready." Not because they aren't qualified but because they've been conditioned to question themselves or conditioned to wait for a stamp of approval that may never come.

I have seen this over the years of working with hundreds of women by way of web design services, coaching programs, events, and podcast interviews—women who are brilliant, capable, called, and chosen yet holding back because no one has ever handed them the mic and said, "It's your turn." So, they play small.

They edit themselves. They wait for perfect timing, perfect graphics, or perfect confidence.

Let me say it clearly: *Your potential isn't waiting to be created. It's waiting to be claimed.*

You get to validate yourself. You get to declare that what's inside of you is worthy of being seen, heard, and experienced by the world. You don't need another certificate, another degree, or another nod of approval to walk boldly in your purpose.

Here's why: The world doesn't benefit from your hidden light. It benefits when you show up and operate in your purpose and expertise—when you finally say, "I see me. I believe in my potential. I choose to show up for me."

So, if you've been waiting for someone to validate you, let this be the moment. I'm telling you right now: You are gifted, graced, and fully equipped. Your brilliance is not a someday thing. It's a *today* thing.

Now go activate it!

Activating Potential

Potential alone isn't power. It becomes power when you activate it.

Here's the truth: *You can't just think your way into your next level— you have to move.*

Activation requires both *action* and *alignment*. You can have the vision board, the master plan, and the perfectly curated Instagram bio, but if you don't take action and if your action isn't aligned with clarity, you'll stay stuck. Potential sits idle until it's partnered with movement.

And let me be clear: Activation isn't a mood—it's a decision. A decision to show up before the applause, to trust your voice before the validation, and to take shaky, imperfect steps.

Let me tell you a story: During my time in corporate America, I had a role that was responsible for working in an employee resource center. Employees of the company could come to the resource center for self-development, training courses, or to talk to a learning consultant.

A young lady scheduled an appointment to have her résumé reviewed because she kept applying for internal positions (so she saw her potential), but she was not getting any job offers. Before her appointment, I reviewed her information and résumé. On paper, she looked like a dream hire for the positions she was going after—I'm talking about degrees, experience, and a good performance record. I was scratching my head. She kept getting overlooked for the very roles she was qualified for. Why?

When she walked in, it became pretty clear that on paper she was awesome but in person her confidence seemed low. Because when it came time to *speak up*, when it came time to *own her value*, she shrunk. She didn't see herself the way her résumé did. Her voice would waver in interviews. She'd downplay her strengths, and potential hiring managers could feel and see that.

I remember thinking, *How can I give her confidence?*

Her confidence was the only thing missing in action, and her potential needed to be activated. That requires consistent nurturing internally and externally. This young lady needed to be around people who consistently remind her of her potential until she believed it.

Let me say, every level I've reached was because I surrounded myself with the right people/community, programs, and platforms: Mentors who challenged me. Masterminds who pushed me. Friends who supported me. Podcasts, stages, interviews, and rooms that required me to rise. But I had to say *yes* to those things before they showed results.

If you don't believe in your own skills, it doesn't matter how talented you are, your confidence will always cap your capacity. So let me offer you three ways to activate your potential from the lens of inner work that transforms outer success:

1. Confront the inner critic. Your greatest obstacle isn't the Facebook algorithm, the saturated market, or even the economy. It's the voice in your head that says, *Who do you think you are?*

Every time you hesitate to show up online, charge for the value you deliver, or share your story, it's not a lack of ability. It's often a lack of internal permission. That's the inner critic at work. Confidence begins when you start challenging the narratives that no longer serve you.

Activation Tip: Ask yourself, "Is this hesitation based on truth or on an old story I've outgrown?" Replace doubt with your data, and look at your results, your client wins, your resilience. You are more capable than that inner voice gives you credit for.

2. Let confidence lead before clarity fully shows up. I always tell clients that you only need fifty-one percent confidence, even if you still have forty-nine percent fear.

Many people are waiting on perfect clarity before taking the next step. But clarity is often a byproduct of movement and not a prerequisite. Confidence is a muscle that gets stronger as you use it. It's built through repetition, exposure, and permission to evolve. Clarity is what develops along the way.

I've seen women who had everything in place—credentials, results, even a following—but they couldn't activate their next level because they were waiting to "feel ready." But here's the truth: We are never really ready for big moves in life, and readiness is a choice, not a feeling.

Activation Tip: Stop asking "Am I ready?" and start saying "I'm showing up anyway." Confidence is a decision. Clarity will meet you on the path.

3. Design your environment to match your identity. This one's psychological. You can't activate your potential if your environment keeps reinforcing your past. That means your relationships, your calendar, your digital space, and even your inner dialogue should reflect the future version of you. Confidence grows when we are surrounded by alignment. Environments that challenge us, affirm us, and stretch us will activate the best in us.

Activation Tip: Audit your space—physical, emotional, relational. Ask, "Does this version of my business reflect the level I'm stepping into?" If not, it's time to shift the atmosphere.

Prioritizing Potential

Me (frantically calling my mother): "Where are you?"

Mom: "I am at Gate A6."

Flashback to thirty minutes prior (like they do in the movies).

My mother and I were traveling from the Hartsfield-Jackson International Airport in Atlanta back to Richmond, Virginia. We were both flying first class, but I have TSA PreCheck, and she does not. When we got to security, she went to the main security checkpoint, and I went to the TSA PreCheck side.

She has metal in her back from a past surgery, so she usually gets pulled over at the metal detectors, which she hates. I thought for sure that I would finish first and wait for her on the other side of security.

After going through the security checkpoint, you enter the main terminal area called the transportation mall. This is where you board the "plane train" for a fast underground train that connects all the concourses. All of the security lines funnel here in this area before boarding the trains.

The Confidence Activator

So here I am ready to board the train to go to concourse A to get to our gate, and my mother is nowhere to be found. I waited patiently and kept looking up the escalator at all of the people filing in from all security checkpoints. My first thought was that the main security line must have been really long and they probably pulled her at the metal detector to do the normal pat down. I went and asked an airport worker if my mom could have gone somewhere else—liked used the elevator instead of the escalator—and the airport worker said no, she would still end up here. I texted my mom, and there was no response.

I called my mom two or three times, and on the third ring, she answered.

Me: "Where are you?"

Mom: "I am at Gate A6."

Me: "How did you get to the gate passed me?"

Mom: "Because I was a first-class traveler, they have a special priority lane in the main security area, and I just walked through, boarded the train to concourse A, and walked to our gate.

So here I was with TSA PreCheck and as a first-class traveler, and my mom still beat me to the gate because the main security checkpoint *prioritized* her service as a first-class traveler.

I fly first class, not because I am bougie (well, maybe a little bit) but because I am a tall and thick sister. I don't want my hip on your hip, so I pay extra mainly for the legroom and wider seats. But here's what else comes with that: priority service. I get to check in my bag first. I get to board the plane first. I get something to drink or eat first. I get off the plane first. My luggage comes off the conveyor belt first. When you pay for first class, you pay to be their priority.

That's how we need to treat our potential, like it is a priority. When we prioritize our potential, we will reach it faster and quicker.

Women often prioritize tasks, clients, family, careers, and other people's feelings but not their own potential. It does not mean that the other things don't matter because they do. It's just time for you to push your potential to the top of the list and make it a priority.

Below are five expert-level action steps to move you in this direction.

Five Action Steps to Prioritize Your Potential

1. Audit where your energy is going. Take an honest inventory of your time, focus, and emotional bandwidth. If your calendar reflects everyone else's goals but not your own, a change needs to happen. Prioritizing your potential means restructuring your schedule to support your future self, not just your current obligations. This step may not happen overnight, so give yourself grace.

Ask Yourself: "What am I giving energy to that no longer reflects where I'm going?"

2. Design boundaries that protect you. You can't create at a high level while operating in burnout. Prioritize your potential by building boundaries that honor your capacity. That includes learning to say no without guilt and carving out me time and CEO time each week for strategic thinking, planning, and rest.

Remember: Even though some people view boundaries as roadblocks, they are really bridges to your best self.

3. Invest in environments that hold space for you. Potential flourishes in the right atmosphere. Get in rooms, programs, and communities that feel safe, stretch your thinking, normalize excellence, nourish your confidence, and reflect the version of you you're becoming. That might be a coaching program (like my marketing coaching program, The Platform Builder® Program), mastermind, or a first-class seat on the plane. Elevation starts with exposure.

Growth Tip: Prioritizing your potential requires leaving comfort zones and stepping into clarity zones.

4. Decide what you're no longer delaying. Delayed decisions keep potential on pause. Most of the time, delays are wrapped in procrastination, which is rooted in fear.

Identify the one big move you've been avoiding. Perhaps it is launching the brand, raising your prices, applying for the opportunity, submitting that contract. Put it on your priority list this month. The longer you delay, the longer you deny your next level.

Coaching Challenge: Declare the one big move, put a date on when you are going to make the big move, and do it. Send me an email and let me know—info@mitchell-productions.com.

5. Align your platform with the life you're building. Your potential isn't just about hustle—it's about alignment. Is your personal brand, your message, your pricing, and your positioning in sync with your goals? Prioritize your potential by designing a business and brand that reflects who you are *and* where you're going.

Here's what I want you to know: Your potential is not some far-off version of you. It's not waiting on more qualifications or more time. It's waiting on a decision. Prioritizing your potential is strategic. Just like that first-class traveler, you deserve to walk in rooms, board opportunities, and build a life that puts your purpose in priority position. This is your Group 1 boarding call. Your future is at the gate, and it's time to get moving.

As We Wrap Up...

When you *see* your potential, you reclaim the passion that may have been overlooked or unspoken. You stop asking for permission and start owning your power. You realize that you've been walking around with everything you need. You just need to acknowledge it.

When you *activate* your potential, you stop waiting to feel ready and start taking aligned action. You move, even with a little fear in your belly. You get in the room, say yes to every new opportunity, launch the idea, speak up for yourself, and that's when momentum kicks in. Action builds confidence, not the other way around.

And when you *prioritize* your potential, you put your purpose on your calendar. You stop being the last thing on your own to-do list. You build boundaries that protect your growth, say no to what drains you, and align your brand and business with the future you're creating.

Thanks for letting me be your confidence activator over the last few pages. I pass the baton to you now. You are the activator for your own life.

- Start seeing yourself clearly.
- Start moving like it already belongs to you.
- Start putting your potential at the top of the list.
- Start recognizing that fear is a sign that you are leveling up.
- Start believing that you are worthy of all of the goodness you want in life.

Meet the Author | Sharvette Mitchell

Sharvette Mitchell is the CEO of Mitchell Productions, a marketing and professional development firm specializing in personal brand strategy, visibility marketing, and team-building training. With a twenty-five-year background in corporate America at Capital One Bank and a bachelor of science in marketing from Virginia Commonwealth University, Sharvette combines leadership insight with entrepreneurial innovation to help leaders and business owners elevate their visibility and grow their influence and revenue.

She is the visionary behind the trademarked THE PLATFORM BUILDER®—a marketing framework that guides women entrepreneurs and service-based businesses through visibility, marketing, and branding strategies that lead to increased revenue, consistent growth, and recognized authority.

Sharvette delivers this transformation through one-on-one consulting, group coaching programs, strategic team-building sessions, professional development training, and her signature annual conference, The Platform Builder® Summit.

Sharvette is an ICF Professional Certified Leadership Coach, a certified Women-Owned Small Business (WOSB) with the U.S.

Small Business Administration, and SWaM certified by the Virginia Department of Small Business & Supplier Diversity.

Her thought leadership has been featured in *Yahoo! Finance, AARP, Huffington Post, HOPE, CBNation,* and *Sista Sense Magazine.* She has made on-air appearances with CBS 6 *Monday Motivation,* CBS 6 *Virginia This Morning,* The CW Network, and Comcast Cable.

Since 2008, she has hosted *The Sharvette Mitchell Radio Show,* now with more than 775 episodes across major audio and livestream platforms. The show delivers marketing insights and expert conversations that resonate with entrepreneurs, leaders, and changemakers. She was named Radio Personality of the Year by *ACHI Magazine.*

Sharvette is also an eight-time visionary author and book collaboration leader. Her published works include: **PROPEL, POUR, PURSUE, PEARLS, Prepare for PURPOSE, Positioned to PIVOT, PROSPER** and **Prioritize your POTENTIAL,** each project highlighting transformational stories, business insights, and personal growth journeys from women leaders across industries.

She previously served on the board of directors for James River Writers and currently volunteers with International Christian Ministries, Inc., demonstrating her commitment to community engagement and leadership beyond the business world.

Whether she's guiding a small business through a visibility strategy, delivering impactful team-building sessions, or helping leaders find their platform and voice, Sharvette stands at the intersection of marketing, leadership, and purpose-driven success.

Learn more about Sharvette at Mitchell-Productions.com.